KARMIC RELATIONSHIPS

Esoteric Studies

Vol. I

RUDOLF STEINER

Twelve lectures given at Dornach,
Switzerland, from 16th February
to 23rd March, 1924.

Translated by George Adams
with revisions by M. Cotterell, C. Davy
and D. S. Osmond.

Rudolf Steiner Press
London

First Edition 1955
Second Edition 1972
(The revision of the second edition follows that of the
1970 edition in German)
Reprinted 1981

Translated from shorthand reports unrevised by the
lecturer. The original texts of the lectures are contained
in Vol. 1 of the series entitled *Esoterische Betrachtungen
karmischer Zusammenhänge* in the Complete Edition of
Rudolf Steiner's works. (No. 235 in the Bibliographical
Survey, 1961).
This English translation is published in agreement
with the *Rudolf Steiner Nachlassverwaltung*, Dornach,
Switzerland.

ISBN 0 85440 260 8

Printed in Great Britain by The Garden City Press Limited,
Letchworth, Hertfordshire SG6 1JS

In his autobiography, *The Story of My Life* (chapters 35 and 36,), Rudolf Steiner speaks as follows concerning the character of this privately printed matter:

" The contents of this printed matter were intended as oral communications and not for print. . . .

" Nothing has ever been said that was not the purest result of Anthroposophy as it developed. . . . Whoever reads this privately printed matter can take it in the fullest sense as that which Anthroposophy has to say. Therefore it was possible, and moreover without misgivings . . . to depart from the accepted custom of circulating these publications only among the membership. But it will have to be remembered that faulty passages occur in the transcripts which I myself did not revise.

" The right to form a judgment on the content of such privately printed matter can be admitted only in the case of one who has acquired the requisite preliminary knowledge. And in respect of all these publications, this is, at the very least, the anthroposophical knowledge of man and of the cosmos, in so far as it is presented in Anthroposophy, and of what is to be found as ' anthroposophical history ' in the communications from the spiritual world."

SUMMARY OF CONTENTS

VI

How karma enters man's development. Waking and sleeping. Ideation and remembering. Grey and white matter of the brain. In day-consciousness we are incorporated as man; in unconsciousness we are incorporated in the world. Connection of the Hierarchies with head-organisation, rhythmic organisation, motor-sphere. Interweaving of world and the Divine. The Beings of the Third Hierarchy underlie the activity manifested in memory, lead us through the unconscious realm of earthly life. In the life after death the Beings of the Second Hierarchy work on the shaping of inner karma. The Beings of the First Hierarchy, the Creators of the terrestrial, carry out down below the just and compensating activity resulting from our own deeds on earth. This meets us in the next life as facts of destiny. Behind the Law of Karma lie deeds and experiences of the Gods.

2nd March 1924

KARMIC DETERMINATION OF INDIVIDUAL DESTINIES

VII

Representative personalities: Friedrich Theodor Vischer, Franz Schubert, Eugen Dühring, studied biographically.

8th March, 1924

VIII

Karmic connections. Investigations depend on direct vision, and are communicated in narrative form. Arabism and its influence in the 7th, 8th and 9th centuries A.D. Vischer and Hegelianism. Vischer's attitude to Goethe's *Faust.* Schubert and Baron von Spaun. Previous lives of Eugen Dühring. .. ..

9th March, 1924

IX

Details of karmic relationships. How bodily characteristics are carried over from one incarnation into the make-up of the next. Eduard von Hartmann. Friedrich Nietzsche.

15th March, 1924

X

XI

XII

Extract from a lecture given by Rudolf Steiner at Dornach, 22nd June, 1924.

The study of problems connected with karma is by no means easy and discussion of anything that has to do with this subject entails—or ought at any rate to entail—a sense of deep responsibility. Such study is in truth a matter of penetrating into the most profound relationships of existence, for within the sphere of karma and the course it takes lie those processes which are the basis of the other phenomena of world-existence, even of the phenomena of nature. Without insight into the course taken by karma in the world and in the evolution of humanity it is quite impossible to understand why external nature is displayed before us in the form in which we behold it. . . .

What has been said in the lectures here since the Christmas Foundation Meeting should not really be passed on to any audience otherwise than by reading an exact transcript of what has been said here.

A free exposition of this particular subject-matter is not possible at the present stage. If such a course were proposed I should have to take exception to it. These difficult and weighty matters entail grave consideration of every word and every sentence spoken here, in order that the *limits within which the statements are made shall be absolutely clear.* . . .

In the fullest meaning of the words, a *sense of responsibility in regard to communications from the spiritual worlds* begins the moment things are spoken of in the way we are speaking of them now. It is in any case very difficult to speak about these matters here in view of the limitations of our present organisation which do not, however, admit of any other arrangement. It is difficult to speak about these things because such lectures ought really to be given only to listeners who attend the series from beginning to end. Understanding will inevitably be difficult for anyone who comes in later.

If, however, friends are fully conscious that such difficulties exist, a certain balance can be established. Provided this consciousness is present, then all will be well. But it is not always there. . . .

I think that the meaning of what I have said will be understood. I have spoken as I have in order that the necessary earnestness may prevail in regard to lectures of the kind now being given. . . .

I

I now wish to begin to speak to you of the laws and conditions of human destiny, which, as you know, it has become customary to describe as karma. Karma, however, cannot be seen clearly unless we are prepared to learn to know the different kinds of universal law and universal activity. Therefore let me begin by speaking to you in a rather more abstract way of the different kinds of universal law and working, and later crystallise out, as it were, that special kind of working which can be called human destiny or karma.

Both when we try to comprehend the world's phenomena and when we wish to understand the phenomena of human life, we are wont to speak of " causes and effects." Especially in science nowadays, people are accustomed to speak quite generally of " causes and effects." Yet it is precisely this habit which leads into the greatest difficulties, in face of the true reality. For if we speak in this way, we are leaving out of account the *variety* of forms in which " cause and effect " actually occur in the universe.

To begin with we may observe the so-called *lifeless* Nature, which confronts us most clearly of all in the mineral kingdom. There are the marvellous forms which often meet us in the rocks and stones of the earth. There too is all that appears as though it were ground down to powder and compressed again into amorphous stone.

Let us consider, to begin with, all that thus appears to us as the lifeless in the world. When we consider the lifeless purely as such, we find invariably that we can seek within the lifeless itself whatever causes are at work in the lifeless realm. Wherever there is anything lifeless as an effect, there too—within the realm of the lifeless—we may look for the causes. And indeed, we only proceed according to true science if we do this—if we seek within the lifeless kingdom the causes of all lifeless processes.

11

However beautifully formed the crystal which you have before you, you must investigate its forms within the lifeless realm. This means that the lifeless kingdom is really self-contained. We may not be able to say, to begin with, where we shall find its bounds. They may be very far away in cosmic distances. Nevertheless, whatever lifeless process or effect confronts us, if we are looking for its causes, we must seek them—once again—within the realm of the lifeless.

Therewith, however, we are already placing the lifeless side by side with something else, and at once a certain perspective is opened out to us. Consider man himself—how he passes through the gate of death. All that was working and living in him before he went through the gate of death, has vanished from the tangible and visible form which remains behind when the soul passes on. Indeed, we say of this human shape which is left behind, that it is lifeless. Just as we speak of the lifeless when we look out over the rocks and mountains with their crystal forms, so must we speak of the lifeless when we behold the corpse of man, bereft of soul and spirit. And it is only from this moment that we can apply to the human body what applies to the rest of lifeless Nature from the outset.

For those effects which happened in and about the human form during life—before the soul had passed through the gate of death—we could not seek the causes within the lifeless realm. Not only that when a human being lifts his arm we shall look in vain within the lifeless-physical principles of the human form for the causes of the lifting of the arm. Moreover, in the physical-chemical laws which are present in the human form, we shall look equally in vain for the causes— let us say—of the heart-beat, the circulation of the blood, or any other, even involuntary process.

The moment this human form has become a corpse however, the moment the soul has passed through the gate of death, we also observe an effect in the human body. The colour changes in the skin, the limbs become inert—in short, all the effects appear that we are accustomed to witness in the corpse. Where shall we seek the cause ? Within the corpse

12

itself—in the chemical and physical, lifeless laws of the corpse.

Think to the end, in all directions, what I am indicating (for I am doing no more than indicate it), and you will say to yourself: As to his corpse, man, when his soul has passed through the gate of death, has become equal to lifeless Nature. Henceforth we must seek the causes of the effects in the same realm in which the effects themselves are.

This is very important, but precisely when we envisage this characteristic of the human corpse, we find another very significant fact. At death, the human being, so to speak, lays aside his body. Observe with the necessary spiritual faculties what the real man—the man of soul and spirit—has now become, and you will say: The corpse has now been laid aside. For the real man of soul and spirit, having arrived beyond the gate of death, this corpse has no longer significance. It has been cast aside.

For outer lifeless Nature it is quite different. Observe even superficially, and you perceive the difference. Look at a human corpse. You can observe it best where it is buried—so to speak—in the air. Certain communities used to use underground caverns as burial-places, and we there find human corpses simply suspended in the air. They dry until they are completely rotten; you only need to touch them slightly, and they fall asunder into dust.

The " lifeless " which we thus obtain is different from what we find as lifeless Nature all around us. The latter contains a formative, configurative process, giving rise to crystal shapes. Moreover it is in constant change. Apart from the earthy element as such, if we observe the water and the air—which are also lifeless—we find it all in mobility and metamorphosis and transformation.

Nevertheless, let this be placed before our souls at the outset: the equivalence of the human body as to its lifeless nature, after the soul has laid it aside, with the lifeless world of Nature outside of man.

And now we may go farther. Study the *plant* kingdom. Here we come into the sphere of living things. Study the

13

plant in a real way, and we shall find that we are never able to account for the effects merely from causes which lie within the plant kingdom—in the same kingdom where the effects occur. No doubt, there is a science nowadays which tries to do so, but it is in a blind alley! It is at last obliged to say: " We can investigate the physical and also the chemical forces and laws at work in the plant. Something is then left over. . . ." And at this point they diverge, so to speak, into two parties. On the one hand are those who say: " What is left over is a mere synthesis—a kind of form. The physical and chemical laws are the sole effective principle." " No," say the others, " there is something more, which science has not yet discovered, but it will do so no doubt in time."—They will go on speaking like this for a long while yet. For it is not so. If you wish to make research into the plant kingdom you cannot understand it without summoning the whole universe to your aid. You must perceive that the forces for the plant-activity lie in the wide universe. All that takes place in the plant is an effect of the great universe. Before any effects can take place in plant-life, the sun must come into a certain position in the universe. And other forces too must work from the wide universe, to give the plant its form, its inner forces of growth and so on.

Now, if we were able—not in a Jules Verne-fashion, but in reality—to travel say to the moon or to the sun, there too we should not be much wiser in our quest of causes than we are on earth, if we acquired no other faculties of knowledge than those we now possess. We should not reach our goal merely by saying, " Well and good: the causes of effects occurring in the plant kingdom of the earth are not to be found in this kingdom on the earth itself. Let us therefore go to the sun; there we shall find the causes." No, not at all, there too we shall not find them with the ordinary faculties of knowledge. We find them however when we work our way up to Imaginative Cognition—i.e. when we possess quite a new faculty of knowledge. But then we do not need to travel to the sun; we find them in the earth-domain itself. Only we have to pass from " one world " into another; from the everyday physical

14

into the etheric, the ether-world. In the wide universal spaces on every hand, the cosmic ether with its forces is working. It works inward from the wide spaces. The ether is working in on every hand, from the wide spaces.

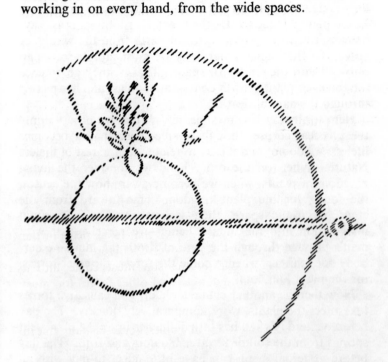

Thus, if we wish to find the causes of the effects in the plant in this kingdom, we must actually pass into a second realm of the universe.

Now man also partakes in what the plant partakes in. The forces working into the plants out of the ether-world, work also into man. Man carries in himself the etheric forces, and we describe the sum-total of these etheric forces which he carries within him, as the human ether-body. I have already told you how the ether-body goes on expanding for a few days after man's death, and how at last it loses itself, so that the human being remains over only in his astral body and his Ego-being.

That which man carried with him etherically, becomes ever larger and larger and loses itself in world-wide distances.

And now once more: compare what we can see of man after his passage through the gate of death, with that which we see in the plant kingdom. Of the plant kingdom we must say: its causative forces come in to the earth from the widths of space. Of the human ether-body we must say: its forces go outward into the widths of space. That is, they go whence the forces of plant-growth come—as soon as man has passed through the gate of death.

Here it already becomes clearer. When we observe only the physical corpse, though we recognise that it becomes lifeless, we do not find it easy to relate it to the rest of lifeless Nature. When on the other hand we consider the living kingdom of plants, when we become aware how the causes, the forces for the plant-kingdom come inward from the ether of cosmic space, then—as we enter with spiritual imagination into the human being—we perceive that with man's passage through the gate of death the human ether-body goes thither, whence come the forces, the ether-forces, for the plant kingdom.

Now there is another characteristic. The causative forces that affect the plants, work comparatively quickly. The day before yesterday's sun has little influence upon the plant as it springs from the soil or receives blossom and fruit. The day before yesterday's sun can have little effect to-day with all its causes. To take effect to-day, it must shine to-day. This point is important; mark it well. You will presently see how important it is.

The plants with their etheric causes have, it is true, their actual fundamental forces within the earthly realm, but they have them in the universe *simultaneously* with the earth.

And when man as a soul-and-spirit being has passed through the gate of death, when the human ether-body dissolves, this again lasts but a short time—only a few days. Here again you have simultaneity. For the duration of the world-process, the few days are a mere trifle. Thus, when the human ether-body returns to where the forces for plant

16

growth—the ether-forces—come from, we can say: As soon as man is living in the ether, his etheric activity is not restricted to the earth (for on the contrary, it leaves the earth), nevertheless, it develops simultaneously. Hence I may write you this scheme:

Mineral Kingdom; Simultaneity of causes and effects within the physical.

Yes, you will say, but surely the causes of some things that take place in the physical are antecedent in time. No, it is not so in reality. For any effects to arise in the physical, the causes must continue working. As soon as the causes cease working, no more effects will occur. Thus we can truly write:

Mineral Kingdom; Simultaneity of causes, within the physical.

And when we come into the plant kingdom (and the same will apply to the plant-nature which we can trace in man himself), there we have simultaneity in the physical and in the superphysical, so we may write:

Plant Kingdom; Simultaneity of causes in the physical and superphysical.

Now let us approach the animal kingdom. In the *animal* kingdom we shall investigate in vain within the animal itself the effects that occur during the creature's life. If it no more than crawls along in search of food—in the physical and chemical processes to be found within its body we shall seek in vain for the causes of these effects. We shall also seek in vain in the wide ether-spaces, where we find the causes for plant-nature. There too we shall look in vain for the causes of animal movement and animal sensation. For all that is plant-like in the animal and in its processes, we shall find the causes in the etheric spaces. And when it dies, the ether-body of the animal too goes outward into the wide universal ether. But for sensation we shall never find the causes within the realms of the earthly-physical, nor of the superphysical and etheric. We shall not find them there.

Here, even more, we come to a point where the modern idea is following up a blind alley. Indeed to some extent it has to admit it. For many a phenomenon that occurs in the

17

animal—all the phenomena of sensation, movement, etc.—
we must admit: If we investigate the physical and chemical
forces within the animal, we cannot find the causes. And in
the cosmic spaces—in the ether-spaces of the universe—there
too we cannot find the causes. If I would explain a flower I
must go out into the widths of the ether-cosmos. Out of the
ether-universe I shall be able to explain the flower. Likewise
I shall be able to explain many things that are plant-like in the
animal. But I shall never be able to explain, even from the
ether-universe, that which occurs in the animal as movement
and sensation.

Suppose I observe an animal on the 20th June. For its
sensation processes, I shall not find the causes on the 20th
of June—not if I seek through all the realms of space within
the earthly realm and beyond. And if I go farther back, there
too I shall not find them—neither in May, nor in April.. . . .

Modern science even feels that it is so. Hence it explains
some at least of what is thus unexplainable, by referring it to
"heredity," that is, by a word. It is "inherited." It comes
down from the ancestors. Not of course everything (that
would be too grotesque), but much of it—it is simply
"inherited."

What is the meaning of this phrase? In the last resort, the
concept of heredity amounts to this: All that confronts us in
the animal, with all its manifold configurations, was poten-
tially contained in the germ-cell of the mother-animal. Such
is the effort of modern science: to study the ox externally, in
the untold variety of its forms, and then to say: The ox comes
from the germ-cell. There were already the forces which in
their full growth and development have given rise to the ox.
Accordingly, the germ-cell is an extremely complex body. . . .
It would indeed have to be appallingly complex, this germ-
cell of the ox. For it would have to contain all that presses
and moulds and twists and turns and works so that the tiny
germ-cell may become the ox with its manifold forms.

However you may twist and turn it (and there are many
theories—evolution, epigenesis, and so on. . . .) however you
may twist it, it comes to this. In the last resort you must

conceive the germ-cell, the minute ovum, as appallingly complicated. And where all things are referred to molecules, supposed to be built up in great complication from the atoms, some scientists are prone to represent the first rudiment of the germ-cell as a complex molecule. But this, my dear friends, does not even accord with physical observation.

Is the germ-cell really a molecule or an organism so complicated? Its peculiar quality lies not at all in complication, but on the contrary: it throws all the matter back into chaos. The germ-cell of all things, in the mother-body, is not a complicated structure, but a material utterly pulverised—chaoticised. It is not organised at all. It is something that falls back into an utterly unorganised, pulverised condition. Never could reproduction take place if it were not for this. Precisely in the egg, unorganised, lifeless matter—which tends to crystalline formation—falls back into complete chaos. Albumen is not the most complicated body, but the very simplest, entirely void of inherent determination. Out of this tiny chaos which the germ-cell is to begin with, no ox could ever arise—no, not in all eternity. For it is really chaos.

Why then does it become the ox? Because at this stage the whole universe proceeds to work upon the germ-cell in the mother organism. Precisely inasmuch as it has become chaos—void of determination in itself—the entire universe can work upon it. Fertilisation has no other object in the world than to reduce matter again to chaos, to the indeterminate void, so that no other entity is working but the pure universe.

But now if we look within the mother-body—there are not the causes. If we look outside into the universal ether—there too, in what takes place simultaneously, are not the causes. We must go back, before the animal came into being, if we would find the causes of what is germinating there as the beginning of a creature capable of sensation and movement. We must go back, before the creature's life began. For all that is capable of sensation and movement, the world of

19

causes lies not in the simultaneous, but *before* the creature's origin.

If it is a plant which I observe, I must go out into the simultaneous, although in the far and wide universe. There I shall find the cause. But if I want to find the cause of all that works as sensation or capacity of movement in the animal, I can no longer go into the simultaneous universe. I must go into that which precedes the creature's life. In other words, the constellation of the stars must have become different. What influences the specifically animal nature is not the constellation in the universe simultaneous with the animal, but the constellation of the stars preceding the animal's life.

Here again, let us turn our thoughts to man after his passage through the gate of death. When he has passed the gate of death, when he has laid aside his ether-body which goes into the wide cosmic spaces—to every place whence come the ether-forces of plant-growth—man must go backward, as I have told you, until his birth. When he has done so, then he has undergone, in backward progress in his astral body, all that he underwent during his life. Thus, with his astral body after death, he has not to enter what is simultaneous, but he must wend his way back to the pre-natal. He must go thither, whence come the forces which provide the animal with faculties of movement and sensation. They do not come from the realm of space, but from the constellations which are simultaneous; they come from the antecedent constellations of the stars. If therefore we are speaking of the animal kingdom, we can no longer speak of simultaneity of causes in the physical and superphysical; we must refer the *present* effects of the physical to *past superphysical* causes. Thus, for the *Animal kingdom:* Past superphysical causes—present effects.

Once again, we enter the concept of time. To put it trivially, we must go for a walk in time. In the physical world, when we are looking for the causes of things that happen there, we move about in the physical. We do not need to leave the physical. And if we are seeking the causes of anything that is brought about in the living kingdom of

20

plants, we must go very far away. We must sweep through the ether-world, and only where the ether-world is at an end—where, as in fairy-tale language, we come to the end of the world—there do we find the causes of plant-growth. But we can wander there as we will; we shall not find there the causes of the faculties of sensation or of movement. To do so, we must set out on a pilgrimage in time. We must go backward in time. We must go out of space, and into time.

As to causation, therefore, we can place the human physical body in its lifeless condition side by side with external lifeless Nature. And we can place the human ether-body—both in its life and in its outward passage after death into the ether-spaces—side by side with the etheric life of the plants; for this too comes in from the ether-spaces, though from the simultaneous constellations, of that which is beyond the physical, above the earth. Moreover, we can relate the human astral body to the outer animal world.

Now, when in further progress from mineral nature to plant and animal, we come at length to the human kingdom proper, perhaps you will say, " We have already considered it." Yes, but not altogether. We have considered it inasmuch as the human being has a physical body; then inasmuch as he has an ether-body; and thirdly, inasmuch as he has an astral body. But you will recognise: if man merely had his physical body, he would be a crystal—even if perhaps a very complicated one. And if in addition he only had his ether-body, he would be a mere plant—no matter, perhaps, how beautiful. And if he even had the astral body added, then he would go on all fours; he would have horns, or the like; in a word, he would be an animal. All this, he is *not*. He has the form and figure he possesses as an upright-walking being, because he also possesses the Ego-organisation, over and above the physical, etheric and astral. To this being alone, who also has the organisation of the Ego, we can apply the name: human kingdom.

Let us observe once more what we have already seen. If we are seeking the causes for the physical, we can remain within the physical. If we are seeking the causes for plant-nature, we must go out into the wide ether-realms. We can still remain within space—though, as I said, this "space" becomes a little hypothetical, so that we have recourse to fairy-like conceptions, as when we say "the end of the world —where the world is boarded up." Yet it is so. Why, even they who only think along the lines of present-day research are now beginning to divine that in some sense there is such a thing as the end of the world—" where the world is boarded up." It is of course a childlike and crude expression. But we need only remember the childlike way in which people are wont to think: There is the sun, it sends out its rays, on and ever on. The rays grow weaker and weaker, it is true, yet the light goes on and on, ever away, into the infinite.

To those who have been at these lectures for years past, I have long ago explained what nonsense it is to imagine that the light goes on and on in this way, into the endless void. Often and often I have said, the expansion of light is subject to a kind of elasticity. If you have an indiarubber ball and you indent it here—you can continue pressing up to a certain point; then it springs back again. There is an end to the elastic pressure; then it recoils. It is the same for the light: it does not go on and out into the endless void. When it has reached a certain limit, it comes back again.

This very idea—that the light does not go on indefinitely, but to a certain limit, whence it returns—has recently been upheld, for example, in England, by the physicist Oliver Lodge. Thus, even outer science has come to the point of maintaining in this instance what is declared by spiritual science; as indeed, in time to come, it will arrive in every detail at the things which spiritual science expounds.

So likewise we may say: Out there, if we think our way far enough outward, sooner or later we must think back again. We must not assume a mere endless space which is a fantasy and moreover, one which we cannot grasp. Some of you may recall what I related in my autobiography of the deep impression it made on me, when I attended classes on modern Synthetic Geometry, and when for the first time it was shown me through Geometry itself that a straight line should not be conceived as though it went out into the endless void and never ceased. The line that goes outward in this direction, actually returns from the opposite side. Geometry expresses it by saying that the infinitely distant point to the right is identical with the infinitely distant point to the left. This can be found by exact calculation—not by the mere analogy of a circle, where, if you set out from here, you will eventually get back again to the same point, and if you then imagine the diameter infinitely long the circle will become a straight line. That would be a mere analogy, of little or no value to one who can think exactly. I was impressed, not by this trivial analogy, but by the possibility of real arithmetical proof, that the infinitely distant point on the one side—to the left—is the same as the infinitely distant point to the right. So that one who begins to run from here and runs on and on along the line will not run out into the endless void; if he only runs on for long enough, he will come back to meet us from the other side. To physical thinking it may seem grotesque. The moment we set aside physical thinking it is a reality. The world is not endless. As physical world, such as it lies before us here, it is limited.

Once more then, we may say: To deal with the plant-nature and with the etheric nature in man, we must go to the very limits of the ether. But if we wish to explain the animal nature, and the astral in man, we must go right outside all that there is in space. We must go for a walk, in time—beyond all that is contemporaneous; we must move forward in time. And now we come to the human kingdom.

When we thus come into time, you see, we are already transcending the physical in a twofold way. In order to describe the animal you must move on in time. But at this stage you must not abstractly pursue the line of thought; you must continue concretely. I beg you now observe, how we continue the line of thought concretely.

People think, when the sun sends out its light, that the light goes endlessly on and on. Oliver Lodge, however, shows that this kind of thought is already beginning to be left behind. They are beginning to realise that you get to a certain limit and thence come back again. The sun receives its light sent

23

back to it again from all directions—though in another form, in a transmuted form, still it receives it back again.

Now let us apply the same kind of thought to the progression we have just followed. We stayed, to begin with, in space. Then, earthly space remained there within, while we must go out into the universe. But even that was not enough, for at the next stage we go out into time. Now, someone might say, we must go on still further—on and on. No, on the contrary; now we *come back again.* Just as it is when we go on and on into space: we get to a limit and thence return; so do we here come back again. Having looked in the distances of time for the past super-physical causes we must return again *into the physical.*

What does this mean in reality? It signifies that out of time we must come down again on to the earth. If we would seek the causes that apply to man as such, we must seek them once more on earth. Only we have gone backward in time, and I need hardly say: when, going backward in time, we come again on to the earth, we come into a former life of man. We come into a former life. For the animal we have to go on and on. It dissolves away in time, just as our ether-body dissolves away to the utmost limits. . . . Man, at this point does not dissolve away; we must come back again, even into his former life on earth. Therefore, in man's case, we can say: Past physical causes, for present effects within the physical.

Mineral kingdom: Simultaneity of causes, within the physical.
Plant kingdom: Simultaneity of causes, in the physical and super-physical.
Animal kingdom: Past super-physical causes, corresponding to present effects.
Human kingdom: Past physical causes, corresponding to present effects in the physical.

You see, it has cost us some pains to-day, by way of preparation, to enter into these abstractions. But that was necessary. I wanted to show you that there is also a logic for these realms—the really spiritual realms of life. This logic is only not coincident with the crude logic which is merely abstracted from physical phenomena, and in which alone people will commonly believe.

Proceeding purely logically, investigating all the series of causes, even in the pure course of thought we came to the repeated lives of man on earth. We need to be attentive to this fact: our thought itself must become different if we would apprehend the spiritual.

People imagine that one cannot understand what is revealed out of the spiritual world. One can indeed, but one must extend one's logic. After all, even to understand a piece of music or any other work of art, you must have in you the conditions to go out to meet it. If you have not the conditions, you will pass by it without appreciation—as a mere noise, if it is music; or if it is plastic art, you will " see nothing in it " but the crude obvious forms. And so for the communications from the spiritual world: you must meet them with a thinking adequate to the spiritual world. And this can already be found in pure logical thinking. Seek out the possible varieties of causes, and you can actually come to understand repeated earthly lives, even in logical consequence.

Now we remain with the great question which is opened up when we consider the corpse. The corpse has become lifeless. External lifeless Nature stands there before us in its crystals and manifold formations. Here the great question arises: How is lifeless Nature related to the corpse of Man ?

Perhaps you will find that it will lead you on a little in a direction tending towards the answer, if you first seize the matter at the second stage. Say to yourselves: I look at the world of plants around me. Out of the wide spaces of the ether-universe, it bears within it the forces to which my own ether-body returns. Away up yonder in the ether-spaces, is the causative principle which gives the plants their origin. There is the realm to which my ether-body goes when it has served my life. Thither I go, whence—from the ether-spaces—all the life of plants wells forth. Thither I go: that is, I am akin to it. In fact, I can even say: something is there, up yonder. Thither my ether-body goes. Thence comes the greening, springing, sprouting world of plants. Yet there is a

25

difference. I give up my ether-body; the plants on the other hand receive the ether for their life and growth. I, after my death, give my ether-body away; give it away as a thing that is left behind. They on the other hand—the plants—receive this ether-body, as that which gives them life. They have their beginning from yonder realm whither I go with my ending. The plants' beginning joins together with the human ether-body's ending.

This will bring near to you the question: Might it not also be so for the mineral, for all the manifold crystal formations? Might I not ask: perhaps this too is a beginning, in contrast to the ending which, of myself, I leave behind as the physical corpse? Perhaps here too, beginning and ending are joined together?

With this question we will close for to-day, my dear friends. To-morrow we shall begin to enter quite thoroughly the question of human destiny—so-called karma. I shall continue about karma. You will no longer have to find your way through such a jungle of abstractions; but you will also perceive that for a certain unfolding of thought this was a necessary preparation.

II

We shall now go forward from the thoughts which were intended to prepare for the explanations of human destiny or karma. From the abstract element of thought we shall go forward to real life. Step by step, we shall bring before our souls the several domains of life into which man is placed, in order to derive from the constituents of life the foundations for a characterisation of karma, of human destiny.

Man, after all, belongs to the whole universe, and in a far wider sense than we are wont to think. He is a member of the universe, and without it he is really nothing. I have often used the comparison with a member of the human body, say a finger. It is a finger as long as it is on the human body; the moment it is cut off from the body, it is no longer a finger. Outwardly, physically, it is still the same; and yet, it is no longer a finger when it is cut off from the human body.

Likewise, man is no longer man if he is lifted out of the universal world-existence. For to this world-existence he belongs, and without it he can neither be looked upon nor understood as man at all.

Now as we saw again in yesterday's lecture, the world-environment of man is naturally divided into distinct regions. There, to begin with, is the lifeless region of the world which in common parlance we call the mineral. We only become like this mineral or lifeless region of the world when we have laid aside our body; when—as regards this body—we have passed through the gate of death. With our true being, we never really become like this lifeless world. Only the bodily form which we have laid aside becomes like it.

Thus, on the one hand, we see that which man leaves behind him in the lifeless kingdom—the physical corpse. And on the other hand, we see the far-spread lifeless universe of Nature, crystalline and non-crystalline. We human beings, as long as we are living on the earth, are quite unlike this mineral world. This too, I have often pointed out. We in our human form are at once destroyed when we are relinquished as corpse to the mineral world. In the mineral world we are dissolved away, that is to say, what holds our form together has nothing in common with the mineral. Even from this fact it is evident that man, as he lives in the physical world, can receive practically no influences from the mineral as such.

By far the widest influences which he does actually receive from the mineral nature come to him via the senses. We see the mineral, we hear it, we perceive its warmth; in short, we perceive it through the senses. Our other relations to the mineral are very slight. You need but think how little of the actual mineral nature comes into relation to us in our earthly life. The salt with which we salt our food is mineral; so are a few other things which we take in with our food. But by far the greater part of the food the human being absorbs comes from the plant and the animal kingdoms. Moreover, what he absorbs from the mineral kingdom bears a remarkable relation to that which he receives of mineral nature through his senses, purely as psychological impressions, namely as sense-perception. In this connection you should again observe an important point which I have often mentioned here. The human brain weighs on the average 1,500 grammes. That is a pretty fair weight. If it pressed with its full weight on the vessels that are underneath it, they would be utterly crushed. It does not press so heavily, for it is subject to a certain law. I described it again a short while ago. When we put a body in a liquid, it loses some of its weight. You can investigate it, if you have a balance. Imagine this vessel of water removed, to begin with. You weigh the body which is suspended here; it has a certain weight. Then put the vessel of water beneath it, so that the body hanging from the beam is steeped in water. Immediately the equilibrium is upset. The beam of the balance goes down on the other side, for the body has become lighter. And if you now investigate how much, it will prove

28

to have become as much lighter as is represented by the weight of the liquid it displaces. That is to say, if the liquid be water, the body—immersed in the water—will become lighter by the amount of weight of the body of water it displaces. It is the well-known principle of Archimedes, who, as I told you, found it when in his bath. He sat in his bath, and found his leg grow lighter or heavier, according as he laid it in the water or lifted it out. Then he exclaimed: " Eureka! " (I have found it).

It is a thing of great importance but important things, too, are sometimes forgotten. For if the art of engineering had not forgotten this principle of Archimedes, probably one of the worst elemental catastrophes of recent times would not have happened as it did, in Italy. Such things arise even in the outer life, owing to the lack of clarity and synthesis in the prevailing science.

Be that as it may, the body loses in weight by the weight of the liquid it displaces. Now the brain is immersed entirely in the cerebro-spinal fluid. It swims in the cerebral fluid.—Here and there, you can already find it recognised in science that man, inasmuch as he is solid, is like a kind of fish. Yes, he is really a fish; for he consists, as to 90 per cent, of a body of water, and in this the solid parts are swimming, like the fish in water.—So, too, the brain is swimming in the cerebro-spinal water; and it thereby becomes so much lighter that it only weighs 20 grammes. The brain only weighs 20 grammes —only with 20 grammes does it press on the surface beneath it. Think what this means; then you will realise how strongly, inasmuch as our brain is floating in the cerebro-spinal fluid, we human beings have the tendency to become free of the earth—and that in an organ of such importance. We think with an organ that is not subject to earthly gravity; we think in direct opposition to earthly gravity. The organ of our thought is first relieved of earthly weight.

Bear in mind the wide range and immense importance of the impressions you receive through your senses, which you confront with your own free will. Think, by comparison, of

29

the minute influences you receive from salt, and other such substances taken as food or condiment. Then you will come to the conclusion that what comes from the mineral kingdom and has a direct influence on man is also as 20 to 1,500 grammes . . . so great is the predominance of what we receive as mere sense-impressions, where we are independent of the stimuli—for our sense-impressions do not take hold of us and rend us. Moreover, those things in us which are still subject to earthly gravity like the mineral condiments or constituents of our food, are generally such as to preserve us inwardly. Salt has in itself a preserving, a sustaining, a refreshing power.

Man, therefore, is on a large scale independent of the surrounding mineral world. He takes into himself from the mineral world only that which has no immediate influence upon his being. He moves in the mineral world freely and independently.

Indeed, my dear friends, if it were not for this freedom and independence in the mineral world, what we call human freedom would not be there at all. The mineral world, we may truly say, exists as the necessary counterpart to human freedom. If there were no mineral world, neither should we be free beings. The moment we rise into the plant-world, we are no longer independent of it. It only seems to us as though we looked out over the world of plants just as we do over the crystals, over the far-spread mineral realm. In reality it is not so. There is the plant-world spread out before us. We human beings are born into the world as breathing, living beings, endowed with a specific metabolism. All this is far more dependent on our environment than the eyes and ears and other organs which convey our sense-impressions. The far and wide expanse of the plant-world lives by virtue of the ether, which pours in on to the earth from all sides. Man, too, is subject to this ether. When we are born and we begin to grow as little children, when forces of growth make themselves felt in us, these are etheric forces. The very forces which enable the plants to grow are living in us as etheric forces. We carry the ether-body within us. The physical body contains our eyes and our ears. .... As I explained just now, this physical body has nothing in common with the remainder of the physical world. This is proved by the very fact that, as the corpse, it falls to pieces in the physical world. But it is quite different with our ether-body. By virtue of the ether-body we are very much related to the world of plants.

Now you must think of this. That which develops in us as we grow, is, after all, connected very deeply with our destiny. Only to choose grotesque and radical examples, we may have grown in such a way as to be short and thick-set, or tall and lanky, as the case may be; or so as to receive this or that shape of nose. In short, the way we grow is not without its influence on our external form. And this is certainly connected, in however loose a way, with our destiny. But our way of growth is expressed not only in these crude externals. If our instruments and methods of investigation were only delicate enough, we should discover that every man has a different composition of the liver, of the spleen, or of the brain. " Liver " is not simply " liver "; it differs—though in its finer aspects, needless to say—in every human being. All this is connected with the same forces which cause plants to grow. As we look out over the plant-bedecked earth, we should be conscious: That which pours in from the wide ether-spaces, causing the plants to grow, works in us human beings too, bringing about the original and native predisposition of each one of us, and this has very much indeed to do with our destiny. For it belongs very deeply to his fate, whether a man receives out of the ether-world this or that constitution of liver, lung or brain. Man sees, however, only the outer aspect of it all. When we look out over the mineral world we see, more or less, what is contained in it. That is why people are scientifically so fond of the mineral world (if, nowadays, one can speak of scientific fondness at all). They like it, because it contains in itself everything they want to find. For the sustaining forces of the plant-world, this is no longer so. You can perceive at once, as I have told you, the moment you rise to Imaginative Cognition, that the

31

minerals are self-contained within the mineral kingdom; such is the nature of the mineral. That which sustains the plant-world does not appear externally at all to everyday consciousness. To find it we must penetrate into the universe more deeply.

What is it then that is working in the plant-kingdom? What is it that is working so that the forces pour in from the wide ether-spaces, causing the plants to spring and sprout from the earth, and in us too, bringing about our growth—the finer composition of our body? What is it that is working? Here, my dear friends, we come to the Beings of the Third Hierarchy, so-called—the Angeloi, Archangeloi and Archai. They are invisible to us, but without them there would not be that ebb and flow of the etheric forces, causing the plants to grow, and working also in ourselves, inasmuch as we too carry in us the same forces which bring about plant-growth. Not to remain obtuse in knowledge, when we approach the plant-world and its forces we can no longer adhere to the merely outward and visible.

And we must also be aware that in the body-free condition between death and a new birth, we develop our relations to these Beings—Angeloi, Archangeloi, Archai. And according to the kind of relations we develop, so does our internal karma take shape: what I might call our nature-karma, that of our karma which depends upon the way our ether-body compounds the living fluids in us, making us grow short or tall, and so forth. . . .

However, the Beings of the Third Hierarchy have only a certain degree of power. It is not owing to their power alone that plants can grow. In this respect, the Third Hierarchy—Angeloi, Archangeloi and Archai—are in the service of higher Beings. Nevertheless, that which we live through before we come down from the spiritual world into our physical body—that which determines the finer constitution of our body—is brought about by our conscious meeting with these Beings of the Third Hierarchy, we having prepared ourselves for this during our former life on earth. With the direction, with the guidance we receive from them to form our ether-body from

32

the wide ether-spaces, all this is achieved shortly before we descend from super-physical into physical existence.

Thus we must first observe that which enters into our destiny or karma out of our own internal constitution. Perhaps we may describe this portion of karma by the terms " well-being " or " comfort " and " discomfort," " content" and " discontent " in life. For our well-being or contentedness or our discontent in life are connected with this inner quality which is ours by virtue of our ether-body. Now there is a second element living in our karma. It depends upon the fact that not only the plant-kingdom but the animal kingdom also, peoples the earth. Think what different kinds of animals there are in the different regions of the earth. The animal atmosphere, so to speak, is different in the one region and the other.

But you will certainly admit that man also lives in this atmosphere in which the animals are living. It may seem grotesque nowadays, but that is only because the people of to-day are unaccustomed to observe such things. For instance, there are districts where the elephant is at home. These are simply the districts where the universe so works down on to the earth that elephant life can arise. Do you suppose, my dear friends—if this be a portion of the earth which the elephant inhabits, where the elephant-creating forces are working in from the cosmos—do you suppose that these forces are absent if a human being happens to be there ? They are still there, needless to say, and so it is with all animal nature. Just as the plant-forming forces from the far ether-spaces are there, wherever we are living (for not wood walls, nor brick, nor even concrete will keep them from us; we here are living in the forces that form the plant-world of the Jura Alps) so, too, if he happens to be in a region where the earth-nature is such that the elephant can have its life, the human being also lives under the elephant-creating forces.

I can very well imagine many a quality of animals, both large and small, living in the souls of men ! There are the animals inhabiting the earth, and as you have now learnt,

33

man lives in the self-same atmosphere. And all this really works upon him. Of course, it affects him differently from how it affects the animals, for man has other qualities than

they; man has additional members of his being. It affects him differently; if it did not, man in the elephantine sphere would also grow into an elephant, which he does not do. Moreover, man constantly raises himself out of these things that work upon him. Nevertheless, he lives in this atmosphere.

All that exists in the human *astral* body is dependent upon the atmosphere in which he lives. And as we said just now that his well-being, his contentment or discontent, depends on the plant-nature of the earth, so may we say at this point: The sympathies and antipathies which we unfold as human beings in our earthly life, and bring with us from the pre-earthly, depend upon the forces constituting, so to speak, the animal atmosphere.

The elephant has a trunk, and thick, pillar-like legs; the stag has antlers and so forth. Here we behold the animal-creating, animal-forming forces. In man, these forces only show themselves in their effect upon his astral body, and it is in their effect upon the astral body that they beget the sympathies and antipathies which every human individual brings with him from the spiritual world.

34

Observe them, my dear friends, these sympathies and antipathies. Observe to what a large extent they guide us throughout life. Undoubtedly, and with good justification in a certain respect, we are brought up and trained so as to grow out of our strong sympathies and antipathies. Yet in the first place they are there. One man has sympathy for this, another man for that; one man for sculpture, another for music; one prefers fair people, another has sympathy for dark people. These are the strong, radical sympathies; but our whole life is pervaded by sympathies and antipathies. In reality they depend for their existence on that which engenders all the variety of animal formations.

Thus you may ask, what do we human beings carry within us, in our own inner being, corresponding to the animal forms that are outside us? They are a hundred- and a thousandfold—these forms. So are the forms of our sympathies and antipathies, only that the greater part remains in our unconscious—or sub-consciousness.

This is another world—a third world. First is the world where we feel no essential dependence—that is the mineral. Second is the world in which Angeloi, Archangeloi and Archai live. That is the world which brings forth the springing, sprouting world of plants, and which endows us with our inner quality whereby we bring well-being or discomfort with us into life, so that we feel, by virtue of our nature, happy or miserable, as the case may be.

Out of this world is taken that which determines our destiny by virtue of our inner constitution—our individual etheric humanity. Now we come to a third element deeply conditioning our destiny, namely our sympathies and antipathies. And, after all, it is through these sympathies and antipathies that many other things are brought into our life, belonging to our destiny in a far wider sense than the sympathies and antipathies themselves. One man is carried into far distances by his sympathies and antipathies. He lives in this or that part of the world because his sympathies have taken him there, and in that distant land, the detailed events of his destiny will now unfold.

Yes, these sympathies and antipathies are deeply involved in all our human destiny. They have their life in the world in which not now the Third but the Second Hierarchy are living: the Exusiai, Dynamis and Kyriotetes. In the animal kingdom lives the earthly image of the sublime, majestic formations of this Hierarchy. And what these Beings implant in *us*, when we commune with them between death and a new birth, lives in the innate sympathies and antipathies which we bring with us from the spiritual world into the physical.

When you see through these things, such ordinary concepts as that of " heredity " appear really very childish. Before I can carry in me any inherited characteristic of my father or mother, I must first have unfolded the sympathies or anti-pathies for this characteristic of father or mother. It does not depend on my having inherited the characteristic by a mere lifeless causality of Nature. It all depends whether I had sympathy for these characteristics.

As to why I had sympathy for them—that is a question we shall deal with in the coming lectures. But to speak of heredity in the way they generally do in modern science is childish, although science thinks itself so clever.

They even speak to-day of the inheritance of specifically spiritual and psychological characteristics. Genius is sup-posed to be inherited from ancestors, and when a man of genius appears in the world, they try to gather up among his forebears the several portions which, they suppose, should produce this genius as a resultant. Well, that is a strange method of proof. A sensible method would be to show that once a man of genius is there, his genius is then transmitted by inheritance. But if they looked for the proof of that, they would come upon very strange things . . . Goethe, too, had a son; and so had other men of genius.

Nevertheless, as I said, that would be the way to prove it. But when a genius is there, to look for certain of his qualities among his forebears is just as though you were to prove that when I fall in the water and am pulled out again, then I am wet. It does not prove that I have much to do, in my essential nature, with the water that is dripping from me.

36

Naturally, having been born into this stream of inheritance through my sympathy for its characteristics, I have them about me, as "inherited characteristics." Just as I have the water about me, when I fall in and am pulled out again. People's ideas in this respect are grotesquely childish. For the sympathies and antipathies already emerge in man's pre-earthly life. They give him his innermost stamp. With them he enters into his earthly life; with them he builds his destiny from the pre-earthly.

Now we can readily imagine: In a former life on earth we were with another human being. Manifold things resulted from our life together, and found their continuation in the life between death and a new birth. . . . There, under the influence of the forces of the Hierarchies, in the living Thoughts and cosmic Impulses, there is fashioned and created what shall pass over from the experiences of our former lives on earth into the next life, to be lived out further. We need the sympathies and antipathies so as to unfold the impulses through which we find one another in life. Formed in the life between death and a new birth, under the influence of Exusiai, Dynamis, Kyriotetes, our sympathies and antipathies enable us to find in life the human beings with whom we must now continue living, according to our former lives on earth. All this takes shape out of the inner structure of our human being. Naturally, manifold errors occur in our acquiring these sympathies and antipathies. Such aberrations, however, are balanced out again in the course of destiny through many lives on earth.

Here, then, we have a second constituent of destiny or karma—the sympathies and antipathies. So we may say:

The first constituent of karma: well-being or inner comfort and discomfort. *The second:* sympathies and antipathies. And, as we come to the sympathies and antipathies in human destiny, we have ascended into the sphere in which lie the forces for the forming of the animal kingdom.

Now, we rise into the human kingdom as such. For we live not only with the plant-world; we live not only with the animal; we live, above all, with other human beings in the

37

world. This is the most important of all for our destiny. That is quite another " living together " than the common life with plants and animals. It is a living-together through which is fashioned what is of main importance in our destiny.

The impulses which bring about the peopling of the earth with human beings, work on humanity alone. So there arises the question, what impulses are these which work only upon humanity ? Here we can let purely external observation tell its tale. It is a course which we have often followed.

Truly, our life is guided—from the other side of it, so to speak—with a far greater wisdom than is ours in guiding it from this side. Often in later life we meet a human being who becomes of extreme importance in our life. When we think back: How did we live until the moment when we met him ? Then our entire life seems like the very pathway to the meeting. It is as though we had tended every step, that we might find him at the right moment—or that we might find him at all, at a certain moment.

We need only ponder the following: Think, my dear friends, what it signifies for fully conscious human reflection. Think what it means to find another human being in a given year of life, thenceforth to experience, work or achieve— whatever it may be—in common with him. Think what it means, think what emerges as the impulse that led up to it, when we reflect on this quite consciously. When we begin to think: How did it happen that we met him ? It will probably occur to us that we first had to experience an event with which many other people were connected, for otherwise the opportunity would not have arisen for us to meet him in this life. And, that this event might happen, we had to undergo still another event . . . and so on. We find ourselves in the midst of the most complex chain of circumstances, all of which had to occur, into all of which we had to enter, so as to reach this or that decisive experience. And now we may perhaps reflect: If the task had been set us—I will not say at the age of one, but let us say at the age of fourteen—to solve the riddle consciously: to bring about in our fiftieth year a decisive meeting with another human being; if we imagine that we had to solve it consciously, like a mathematical problem—think what it would involve!

Consciously, we human beings are so appallingly stupid, whereas what happens with us in the world is so infinitely wise, when we take into account such things as these. When we begin to think along these lines, we become aware of the immense intricacy and deep significance in the workings of our destiny or karma. And this all goes on in the domain of the human kingdom. All that thus happens to us is deep in the unconscious life. Until the moment when a decisive event approaches us, it lies in the unconscious. All this takes place as though it were subject to Laws of Nature. Yet where are the Laws of Nature that have power to bring about such things? For the things that take place in this domain will often contradict all natural law—or all that we elaborate after the pattern of outer natural laws. This, too, I have often mentioned. The external features of human life may even be cast into the framework of mathematical laws.

Take, for example, the life-insurance system. Life-insurance can only prosper inasmuch as one can calculate the probable length of life of any human being, aged, let us say, 19 or 25. If you wish to insure your life, the policy will be made out according to the figure of your probable length of life. As a human being of 19, you will probably live so or so long; this figure can be determined. But now imagine that the allotted time has run its course. You will not feel obliged to die. At the end of their probable length of life, two people may long ago have died. But, on the other hand, they may be long " dead "—according to the insurance-estimate—when they find one another in life in the decisive way I just described. These things transcend what one can calculate for human life from outer facts of Nature and yet they happen with inner necessity like natural facts. We cannot but admit: With the same necessity with which any event of Nature takes place—be it an earthquake, or eruption, or any natural event, whether great or small—with the same necessity two human beings meet in life according to the ways of life which they have taken.

39

Thus we here see established within the physical, another kingdom; and in this kingdom we are living. We live not only in *comfort and discomfort*, in *sympathies and antipathies*, but in this realm also—in our *events and experiences*. We are completely cast into this realm of the events and experiences which determine our life by destiny.

Archai, Archangeloi, Angeloi. 1. Well-being (comfort,
discomfort).

Kyriotetes, Dynamis, Exusiai. 2. Sympathies,
Antipathies.

Seraphim, Cherubim, Thrones. 3. Events, Experiences.

In this realm the Beings of the First Hierarchy—Seraphim, Cherubim, Thrones—are working. To direct all that is working here—every human step, every impulse of soul—to guide it all in the world so that the destinies of men grow out of it, a greater power is needed than works in the plant-kingdom, a greater power than belongs to the Hierarchy of Angeloi, Archangeloi, Archai, or to the Hierarchy of Exusiai, Kyriotetes, Dynamis. It needs a power such as belongs to the First Hierarchy, to the most sublime of Beings: Seraphim, Cherubim and Thrones.

What is lived out in this sphere lives in our true "I", in our Ego-organisation, and it lives over from an earlier earth-life.

Now consider for a moment: you are living in an earth-life. In this earth-life you effect this or that; perhaps you do it out of instinct or passion or a strong impulse, or perhaps it is thought out—either stupidly or cleverly. In any case what you bring to pass is done in accordance with some impulse or other. But now all you do in this way in an earth-life leads to this or that result; it works for the happiness or the harm of some other human being. Then comes the life between death and a new birth. In this life between death and a new birth you have a strong consciousness of the fact: I have done harm to another man, and I am less perfect than I should be had I not done him harm. I must compensate for it. The impulse, the urge arises in you to compensate for the harm you have done. Or again, if you have done something to another that is for his good, that helps him on, then you look upon what you have done and you say to yourself: That must serve to build the foundation for the general good, it must lead to further consequences in the world. All this you can inwardly develop. And it can give you a sense of well-being or of discomfort according as you form the inner nature of your body in the life between death and a new birth. It can lead you to sympathies and anti-pathies, inasmuch as you build and shape your astral body correspondingly, with the aid of the Exusiai, the Dynamis and the Kyriotetes.

All this, however, will not yet give you the power to trans-mute what in a former life was merely a human fact, into a deed of the cosmos. You helped another human being or you harmed him. This must entail his meeting you in a next life on earth, and in the meeting with him you will have to find the impulse to balance-out the deed.

What, to begin with, has only moral significance, must be transformed into an outer fact—an outer event in the world. To do so, those Beings are needed who transmute or metamorphose moral deeds into world-deeds, cosmic deeds. They are the Beings of the First Hierarchy: Seraphim, Cherubim, Thrones. It is they who transmute what goes out from us in one earthly life into our experiences of the next lives on earth. They work in the " events and experiences " in human life.

Here then we have the three fundamental elements of our karma. Our inner constitution, our own internal human nature is subject to the Third Hierarchy. Our sympathies and antipathies (which, as we saw, already became in some sense our environment) are a concern of the Second Hierarchy. And that which we encounter as our actual external life is a concern of the First, the most sublime of the Hierarchies above humanity.

Thus we perceive man's connection with the world and the whole way he stands in it. We come to the great question, how do the many detailed events of his destiny evolve out of these three ?

He is born to such and such parents, in such and such a home, at a certain spot on the earth, into this or that nation, into a given nexus of facts. But all that takes place inasmuch as he is born of such parents, handed over to his educators, born into a certain nation and at a certain spot on earth—all this which enters so fatefully into his life, no matter what we say of human freedom—is in some way dependent on these three elements of which human destiny is composed.

All detailed questions will be revealed to us in their true answers, if we begin with the right foundations. Why does a man get small-pox in his twenty-fifth year, passing through perhaps extreme danger of his life ? How does some other illness or event strike down into his life ? Or some essential help through this or that older person, through this or that nation, this or that series of outer events—how does it come into his life ? In every case we must go back to these, the three constituents of human destiny, whereby he is placed into the totality of the cosmic Hierarchies. It is only in the realm of the mineral world that man moves freely. There is the realm of his freedom.

Only when he becomes aware of this, does he learn to put the question of freedom in the true way. Read my *Philosophy of Spiritual Activity*,* and see how much importance I attach to the point that one should not ask about the freedom of the Will. The Will lies deep, deep down in the unconscious, and it is nonsense to ask about the freedom of the Will. It is only of the freedom of Thoughts that we can speak. I drew the line very clearly in my *Philosophy of Spiritual Activity*. Man must become free in his thoughts, and the free thoughts must give the impulse to the will—then he is free. Now with his thoughts he lives in the mineral world. In all the rest of his being, with which he lives in the plant, in the animal, and in the purely human kingdom, man is subject to destiny. Therefore, of freedom we may truly say: Out of the realms that are ruled by the Hierarchies, the human being comes into that realm which, in a sense, is free from them—into the mineral kingdom, there to become free in his turn. This mineral

* In German: *Philosophie der Freiheit* (freedom).

kingdom—it is precisely the kingdom to which man only becomes similar as to his corpse, when he has laid the corpse aside and passed through the gate of death. Man in his earthly life is independent of that kingdom which can only work to his destruction. No wonder he is free in it, since it has no other part nor lot in him than to destroy him the very moment it gets him. He simply does not belong to this kingdom. Man must first die; then only—as a corpse—can he be, even in outer phenomenal Nature, in the kingdom in which he is free.

Man becomes older and older, and if no accidents occur (these, too, we shall learn to know in their karmic aspects), if he dies as an old man, eventually as a corpse he becomes like the mineral kingdom. As he grows older, so does he gradually come into the sphere of the lifeless. At length he gives up his corpse—it is separated off from him. It is no longer man— needless to say, the corpse is no longer man. Let us look at the mineral kingdom: it is no longer God. Just as the corpse is no longer man, so is the mineral kingdom no longer God. What is it then? The Godhead is in the plant, in the animal, in the human kingdom; for we have found it there in the three Hierarchies. But in the mineral kingdom the God-head is not, any more than the human corpse is man. The mineral kingdom is the corpse of the Divine. However, as we proceed we shall encounter the strange fact—which I shall only hint at now—that whereas man grows older to become a corpse, the Gods grow younger. . . . For they are on the other path, the path which we go through after our death. Therefore the mineral is the youngest of the kingdoms. Yet it is the one which is separated off by the Gods, and for this very reason, man can live in it as in the realm of his freedom.

Such are the real connections. Man learns to feel himself ever more at home in the world when he thus learns to place his sensations, his thoughts, his feelings and impulses of will into the right relation to the world. Moreover, only in this way can he perceive how he is placed by destiny in the world and in relation to other men.

III

Karma is best understood by contrasting it with the other impulse in man—that impulse which we describe with the word *Freedom*. Let us first place the question of karma before us, quite crudely, if I may say so. What does it signify ? In human life we have to record the fact of re-incarnation, successive earthly lives. Feeling ourselves within a given earthly life, we can look back—in thought, at least, to begin with—and see how this present life is a repetition of a number of former earthly lives. It was preceded by another, and that in turn by yet another life on earth, and so on until we get back into the ages where it is impossible to speak of repeated earthly lives as we do in the present epoch of the earth. For as we go farther backward, there begins a time when the life between birth and death and the life between death and a new birth become so similar to one another that the immense difference which exists to-day between them is no longer there at all. To-day we live in our earthly body between birth and death in such a way that in everyday consciousness we feel ourselves quite cut off from the spiritual world. Out of this everyday consciousness men speak of the spiritual world as a " beyond." They will even speak of it as though they could doubt its existence or deny it altogether.

This is because man's life in earthly existence restricts him to the outer world of the senses, and to the intellect; and intellect does not look far enough to perceive what is, after all, connected with this earthly existence. Hence there arise countless disputations, all of which ultimately have their source in the " unknown." No doubt you will often have stood between, when people were arguing about Monism, Dualism and the rest. . . . It is, of course, absurd to argue around these catch-words. When people wrangle in this way, it often seems as though there were some primitive man

who had never heard that there is such substance as " air."
To one who knows that air exists, and what its functions
are, it will not occur to speak of it as something that is
"beyond." Nor will he think of declaiming: " I am a Monist;
I declare that air, water and earth are one. You are a
Dualist, because you persist in regarding air as something
that goes beyond the earthly and watery elements."

These things, in fact, are pure nonsense, as indeed all dis-
putes about concepts generally are. Therefore there can be
no question of our entering into these arguments. I only wish
to point out the significance. For a primitive man who does
not yet know of its existence, the air as such is simply absent;
it is " beyond," beyond his ken. Likewise for those who do
not yet know it, the spiritual world is a " beyond," in spite
of the fact that it is everywhere present just as the air is.
For a man who enters into these things, it is no longer
" beyond " or " on the other side," but " here," " on this
side."

Thus it is simply a question of our recognising the fact:
In the present earthly era, man between birth and death lives
in his physical body, in his whole organisation, so that this
very organisation gives him a consciousness through which he
is cut off from a certain world of causes. But the world of
causes, none the less, is working as such into this physical and
earthly life. Then, between death and a new birth he lives
in another world, which we may call a spiritual world by
contrast with this physical. There he has not a physical body,
such as could be made visible to human senses; he lives in a
spiritual form of being. Moreover, in that life between death
and a new birth the world through which he lives between
birth and death is in its turn as remote as the spiritual world
is remote and foreign for everyday consciousness on earth.

The dead look down on to the physical world just as the
living (that is, the physically living) look upward into the
spiritual world. But their feelings are reversed, so to speak.
In the physical world between birth and death, man has a way
of gazing upward, as to another world which grants him
fulfilment for very many things which are either deficient or

46

altogether lacking in contentment in this world. It is quite different between death and a new birth. There, there is an untold abundance, a fulness of events. There is always far too much happening compared with what man can bear; therefore he feels a constant longing to return again into the earthly life, which is a " life in the beyond " for him there. In the second half of the life between death and a new birth, he awaits with great longing the passage through birth into a new earth-existence. In earthly existence man is afraid of death because he lives in uncertainty about it, for in the life on earth a great uncertainty prevails for the ordinary consciousness about the after-death. In the life between death and a new birth, on the other hand, man is excessively certain about the earthly life. It is a certainty that stuns him, that makes him actually weak and faint—so that he passes through conditions, like a fainting dream, conditions which imbue him with the longing to come down again to earth.

These are but scant indications of the great difference now prevailing between the earthly life and the life between death and a new birth. Suppose, however, that we now go back, say, no farther back than the Egyptian time—the third to the first millennium before the founding of Christianity. (After all, the men to whom we there go back are but ourselves, in former lives on earth.) In yonder time, the consciousness of man during his earthly life was quite different from ours to-day, which is so brutally clear, if you will allow me to say so. Truly, the consciousness of the men of to-day is brutally clear-cut, they are all so clever—I am not speaking ironically—the people of to-day *are* clever, all of them. Compared to this terribly clear-cut consciousness, the consciousness of the men of the ancient Egyptian time was far more dream-like. It did not impinge, like ours does, upon outer objects. It rather went its way through the world without " knocking up against " objects. On the other hand, it was filled with pictures which conveyed something of the Spiritual that is there in our environment. The Spiritual, then, still penetrated into man's physical life on earth.

Do not object: " How could a man with this more dream-like, and not the clear-cut consciousness of to-day, have achieved the tremendous tasks which *were* actually achieved, for instance, in ancient Egypt ? " You need not make this objection. You may remember how mad people sometimes reveal, in states of mania, an immense increase of physical strength; they will begin to carry objects which they could never lift when in their full, clear consciousness. Indeed, the physical strength of the men of that time *was* correspondingly greater; though outwardly they were perhaps slighter in build than the people of to-day—for, as you know, it does not always follow that a fat man is strong and a thin man physically weak. But they did not spend their earthly life in observing every detail of their physical actions; their physical deeds went parallel with experiences in consciousness into which the spiritual world still entered.

And when the people of that time were in the life between death and a new birth, far more of this earthly life reached upward into yonder life—if I may use the term " upward." Nowadays it is exceedingly difficult to communicate with those who are in the life between death and a new birth, for the languages themselves have gradually assumed a form such as the dead no longer understand. Our nouns, for instance, soon after death, are absolute gaps in the dead man's perception of the earthly world. He only understands the verbs, the " words of time " as they are called in German —the acting, moving principle. Whereas on earth, materialistically minded people are constantly pulling us up, saying that everything should be defined and every concept well outlined and fixed by clear-cut definition, the dead no longer know of definitions; they only know of what is in movement, they do not know that which has contours and boundaries.

Here again, it was different in ancient times. What lives on earth as speech, and as custom and habit of thought, was of such a kind that it reached up into the life between death and a new birth, and the dead had it echoing in him still, long after his death. Moreover, he also received an echo of what he had experienced on earth and also of the things that were taking place on earth after his death.

And if we go still farther back, into the time following the catastrophe of Atlantis—the 8th or 9th millennium B.C.—the difference becomes even smaller between the life on earth and life in the Beyond, if we may still describe it so. And thence, as we go backward, we gradually get into the times when the two lives were similar. Thereafter, we can no longer speak of repeated earthly lives.

Thus, our repeated lives on earth have their limit when we go backward, just as they have their limit when we look into the future. What we are beginning quite consciously with Anthroposophy to-day—the penetration of the spiritual world into the normal consciousness of man—will indeed entail this consequence. Into the world which man lives through between death and a new birth, the earthly world will also penetrate increasingly; and yet man's consciousness will not grow dream-like, but clearer and ever clearer. The difference will again grow less. Thus, in effect, our life in repeated incarnations is contained between two outermost limits, past and future. Across these limits we come into quite another kind of human existence, where it is meaningless to speak of repeated earthly lives, because there is not the great difference between the earthly and the spiritual life, which there is to-day. Now let us concentrate on present earthly time—in the wide sense of the word. Behind our present earthly life, we may assume that there are many others—we must not say countless others, for they can even be counted by exact spiritual scientific investigation. Behind our present earthly life there are, therefore, many others. When we say this, we shall recognise that in those earthly lives we had certain experiences—relationships as between man and man. These relationships as between man and man worked themselves out in the experiences we then underwent; and their effects are with us in our present earthly life, just as the effects of what we do in this life will extend into our coming lives on earth. So then we have to seek in former earthly lives the causes of many things that enter into our life to-day.

At this point, many people are prone to retort: " If then the things I experience are caused, how can I be free ? " It is

49

a really significant question when we consider it in this way. For spiritual observation always shows that our succeeding earthly life *is* thus conditioned by our former lives. Yet, on the other hand, the consciousness of freedom is absolutely there. Read my *Philosophy of Spiritual Activity* and you will see: the human being cannot be understood at all unless we realise that the whole life of his soul is oriented towards freedom—filled with the tendency to freedom.

Only, this freedom must be rightly understood. Precisely in my *Philosophy of Spiritual Activity* you will find a concept of freedom which it is very important to grasp in its true meaning. The point is that we have freedom developed, to begin with, in *thought*. The fountain-head of freedom is in thought. Man has an immediate consciousness of the fact that he is a free being in his thought. You may rejoin: " Surely there are many people nowadays who doubt the fact of freedom ? " Yes, but it only proves that the theoretical fanaticism of people nowadays is often stronger than their direct and real experience. Man is so crammed with theoretical ideas, that he no longer believes in his own experiences. Out of his observations of Nature, he arrives at the idea that everything is conditioned by necessity, every effect has a cause, all that exists has a cause. He does not think of repeated earthly lives in this connection. He imagines that what wells forth in human Thinking is causally determined in the same way as that which proceeds from any machine.

Man makes himself blind by this theory of universal causality, as it is called. He blinds himself to the fact that he has very clearly within him a consciousness of freedom. Freedom is simply a fact which we experience, the moment we reflect upon ourselves at all.

There are those who believe that it is simply the nervous system; the nervous system is there, once and for all, with its property of conjuring thoughts out of itself. According to this, the thoughts would be like the flame whose burning is conditioned by the materials of the fuel. Our thoughts would be necessary results, and there could be no question of freedom.

These people, however, contradict themselves. As I have often related, I had a friend in my youth, who, at a certain period, had quite a fanatical tendency to think in a " sound," materialistic way. " When I walk," he said, " it is the nerves of the brain; they contain certain *causes* to which the *effect* of my walking is due." Now and then it led to quite a long debate between us, till at last I said to him on one occasion: " Look now. You also say: ' I walk.' Why do you not say ' My brain walks ? ' If you believe in your theory, you ought never to say: ' I walk; I take hold of things,' and so on, but ' My brain walks; my brain takes hold of them,' and so on. Why do you go on lying ? "

These are the theorists, but there also those who put it into practice. If they observe some failing in themselves which they are not very anxious to throw off, they say, " I cannot throw it off; it is my nature. It is there of its own accord, and I am powerless against it." There are many like that; they appeal to the inevitable causality of their own nature. But as a rule, they do not remain consistent. If they happen to be showing off something that they rather like about themselves, for which they need no excuse, but on the contrary are glad to receive a little flattery, then they depart from their theory.

The free being of man is a fundamental fact—one of those facts which can be directly experienced. In this respect, however, even in ordinary earthly life it is so: there are many things we do in complete freedom which are nevertheless of such a kind that we cannot easily leave them undone. And yet we do not feel our freedom in the least impaired.

Suppose, for a moment, that you now resolve to build yourself a house. It will take a year to build, let us say. After a year you will begin to live in it. Will you feel it as an encroachment on your freedom that you then have to say to yourself: The house is ready now, and I must move in. . . . I must live in it; it is a case of compulsion. No. You will surely not feel your freedom impaired by the mere fact that you have built yourself a house. You see, therefore, even in ordinary life the two things stand side by side. You have

51

committed yourself to something. It has thereby become a fact in life—a fact with which you have to reckon.

Now think of all that has originated in former lives on earth, with which you have to reckon because it is due to yourself—just as the building of the house is due to you. Seen in this light, you will not feel your freedom impaired because your present life on earth is determined by former ones.

Perhaps you will say: " Very well. I will build myself a house, but I still wish to remain a free man. I shall not let myself be compelled. If I do not choose to move into the new house after a year, I shall sell it." Certainly—though I must say, one might also have one's views about such a way of behaving. One might perhaps conclude that you are a person who does not know his own mind. Undoubtedly, one might well take this view of the matter; but let us leave it. Let us not suppose a man is such a fanatical upholder of freedom that he constantly makes up his mind to do things, and afterwards out of sheer " freedom " leaves them undone. Then one might well say: " This man has not even the freedom to go in for the things which he himself resolves upon. He constantly feels the sting of his would-be freedom; he is positively harassed, thrown hither and thither by his fanatical idea of freedom."

Observe how important it is, not to take these questions in a rigid, theoretic way, but livingly. Now let us pass to a rather more intricate concept. If we ascribe freedom to man, surely we must also ascribe it to the other Beings, whose freedom is unimpaired by human limitations. For, as we rise to the Beings of the Hierarchies, they certainly are not impaired by limitations of human nature. For them indeed we must expect a higher degree of freedom. Now someone might propound a rather strange theological theory—to this effect: God must surely be free. He has arranged the world in a certain way; yet he has thereby committed Himself, He cannot change the World-Order every day. Thus, after all, He is un-free.

You see, you will never escape from a vicious circle if you

52

thus contrast the inner necessity of karma and the freedom which is still an absolute fact of our consciousness, a simple outcome of self-observation. Take once more the illustration of the building of the house. I do not wish to run it to death, but at this point it can still help us along the way. Suppose some person builds himself a house. I will not say suppose *I* build myself a house, for I shall probably never do so!—But, let us say, some one builds himself a house. By this resolve, he does, in a certain respect, determine his future. Now that the house is finished, and if he takes his former resolve into account, no freedom apparently remains to him, as far as the living in the house is concerned. And though he *himself* has set this limitation on his freedom, nevertheless, apparently, no freedom is left to him.... But now, I beg you, think how many things there are that you would still be free to do in the house that you had built yourself. Why, you are even free to be stupid or wise in the house, and to be disagreeable or nice to your fellow-men. You are free to get up in the house early or late. There may be other necessities in this respect; but as far as the house is concerned, you are free to get up early or late. You are free to be an anthroposophist or a materialist in the house. In short, there are untold things still at your free disposal.

Likewise in a single human life, in spite of karmic necessity, there are countless things at your free disposal, far more than in a house—countless things fully and really in the domain of your freedom.

Even here you may still feel able to rejoin: Well and good. We have a certain domain of freedom in our life. Yes, there is a certain enclosed domain of freedom, and all around it, karmic necessity. Looking at this, you might argue: Well, I am free in a certain domain, but I soon get to the limits of my freedom. I feel the karmic necessity on every hand. I go round and round in the room of my freedom, but at the boundaries on every hand I come up against limitations.*

Well, my dear friends, if the fish thought likewise, it would be highly unhappy in the water, for as it swims it comes up

* see diagram (p.54).

53

against the limits of the water. Outside the water, it can no longer live. Hence it refrains from going outside the water. It does not go outside; it stays in the water. It swims around in the water, and whatever is outside the water, it lets it

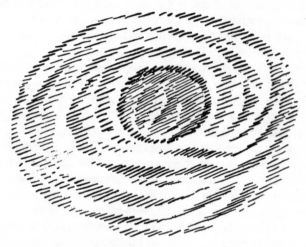

alone; it just lets it be what it is—air, or whatever else. And inasmuch as it does so, I can assure you the fish is not at all unhappy to think that it cannot breathe with lungs. It does not occur to it to be unhappy. But if ever it did occur to the fish to be unhappy because it only breathes with gills and not with lungs, then it would have to have lungs in reserve, so as to compare what it is like to live down in the water, or in the air. Then the whole way the fish feels itself inside, would be quite different. It would all be different.

Let us apply this comparison to human life with respect to freedom and karmic necessity. To begin with, man in the present earthly time has what we call the ordinary consciousness. With this consciousness he lives in the province of his freedom, just as the fish lives in the water. He does not come into the realm of karmic necessity at all, with everyday consciousness. Only when he begins to see the spiritual world (which is as though the fish were to have lungs in reserve)—only when he really lives into the spiritual world—

then he begins to perceive the impulses living in him as karmic necessity. Then he looks back into his former lives on earth, and, finding in them the causes of his present experiences, he does not feel: " I am now under compulsion of an iron necessity: my freedom is impaired," but he looks back and sees how he himself built up what now confronts him. Just as a man who has built himself a house looks back on the resolve which led him to build it. . . . He generally finds it wiser to ask, was it a sensible or a foolish resolve, to build this house ? No doubt, in the event, you may arrive at many different conclusions on this question; but if you conclude that it was a dreadful mistake, you can say at most that you were foolish.

In earthly life this is not a pleasant experience, for when we stand face to face with a thing we have inaugurated, we do not like having to admit that it was foolish. We do not like to suffer from our own foolish mistakes. We wish we had not made the foolish decision. But this really only applies to the one earthly life, because in effect, between the foolishness of the resolve and the punishment we suffer in experiencing its consequences, only the self-same earthly life is intervening. It all remains continuous.

But between one earthly life and another it is not so. For the lives between death and a new birth are always intervening, and they change many things which would not change if earthly life continued uniformly. Suppose that you look back into a former life on earth. You did something good or ill to another man. Between that earthly life and this one, there was the life between death and new birth. In that life, you cannot help realising that you have become imperfect by doing wrong to another human being. It takes away from your own human value. It cripples you in soul. You must make good again this maiming of your soul and you resolve to achieve in a new earthly life what will make good the fault. Thus between death and new birth you take up, by your own will, that which will balance and make good the fault. Or if you did good to another man, you know now that all of man's earthly life is there for mankind as a whole. You see it

55

clearly in the life between death and new birth. If therefore you have helped another man, you realise that he has thereby attained certain things which, without you, he could not have attained in a former life on earth. And you then feel all the more united with him in the life between death and new birth—united with him, to live and develop further what you and he together have attained in human perfection. You seek him again in a new life on earth, to work on thus in a new life precisely by virtue of the way you helped in his perfection.

When therefore, with real spiritual insight, you begin to perceive this encompassing domain, there is no question of your despising or seeking to avoid its necessity. Quite the contrary; for as you now look back on it, you see the nature of the things which you yourself did in the past, so much so that you say to yourself: That which takes place, must take place, out of an inner necessity; and out of the fullest freedom it would have to take place just the same.

In fact it will never happen, under any circumstances, that a real insight into your karma will lead you to be dissatisfied with it. When things arise in the karmic course which you do not like, you need but consider them in relation to the laws and principles of the universe; you will perceive increasingly that after all, what is karmically conditioned is far better—better than if we had to begin anew, like unwritten pages, with every new life on earth. For, in the last resort, we ourselves are our karma. What is it that comes over, karmically, from our former lives on earth ? It is actually we ourselves. And it is meaningless to suggest that anything in our karma (adjoining which, remember, the realm of freedom is always there), ought to be different from what it is. In an organic totality you cannot criticise the single details. A person may not like his nose, but it is senseless to criticise the nose as such, for the nose a man has, must be as it is, if the whole man is as he is. A man who says: " I should like to have a different nose," implies that he would like to be an utterly different man; and in so doing he really wipes himself out in thought— which is surely impossible. Likewise we cannot wipe out our karma, for we are ourselves what our karma is. Nor does it really embarrass us, for it runs alongside the deeds of our freedom; it nowhere impairs the deeds of our freedom.

I may here use another comparison to make the point clear. As human beings, we walk. But the ground on which we walk is also there. No man feels embarrassed in walking because the ground is there beneath him. He must know that if the ground were not there, he could not walk at all; he would fall through at every step. So it is with our freedom; it needs the ground of necessity. It must rise out of a given foundation. And this foundation—it is really we ourselves!

Therefore, if you grasp the true concept of freedom and the true concept of karma, you will find them thoroughly compatible, and you need no longer shrink from a detailed study of the karmic laws. In fact, in some instances you will even come to the following conclusion:

Suppose that some one is really able to look back with the insight of Initiation, into former lives on earth. He knows quite well, when he looks back into his former lives, that this and that has happened to him as a consequence. It has come with him into his present life on earth. If he had not attained Initiation Science, objective necessity would impel him to do certain things. He would do them quite inevitably. He would not feel his freedom impaired, for his freedom is in the ordinary consciousness, with which he never penetrates into the realm where the necessity is working—just as the fish never penetrates into the outer air. But when he has attained to Initiation Science, then he looks back; he sees how things were in a former life on earth, and he regards what now confronts him as a task quite consciously allotted for his present life. And so indeed it is.

What I shall now say may sound paradoxical to you, yet it is true. In reality, a man who has no Initiation Science practically always knows, by a kind of inner urge or impulse, what he is to do. Yes, people always know what they must do; they are always feeling impelled to this thing or that. For one who really begins to tread the path of Initiation Science it becomes very different. With regard to the various experiences of life as they confront him, strange questions

57

will arise in him. When he feels impelled to do this or that, immediately again he feels impelled not to do it. There is no more of that dim urge which drives most human beings to this or that line of action. Indeed, at a certain stage of Initiate-insight, if nothing else came instead, a man might easily say to himself: Now that I have reached this insight— being 40 years old, let us say, I had best spend the rest of my life quite indifferently. What do I care? I'll sit down and do nothing, for I have no definite impulses to do anything particular.

You must not suppose, my dear friends, that Initiation is not a reality. It is remarkable how people sometimes think of these things. Of a roast chicken, every one who eats it, well believes that it is a reality. Of Initiation Science, most people believe that its effects are merely theoretical. No, its effects are realities in life, and among them is the one I have just indicated. Before a man has acquired Initiation Science, out of a dark urge within him one thing is always important to him and another unimportant. But now he would prefer to sit down in a chair and let the world run its course, for it really does not matter whether this is done or that is left undone. . . .

This attitude might easily occur, and there is only one corrective. (For it will not remain so; Initiation Science, needless to say, brings about other effects as well.) The only corrective which will prevent our Initiate from sitting down quiescently, letting the world run its course, and saying: " It is all indifferent to me," is to look back into his former lives on earth. For he then reads in his karma the tasks for his present earthly life, and does what is consciously imposed upon him by his former lives. He does not leave it undone, with the idea that it encroaches on his freedom, but he does it. Quite on the contrary, he would feel himself unfree if he could not fulfil the task which is allotted to him by his former lives. For in beholding what he experienced in former lives on earth, at the same time he becomes aware of his life between death and a new birth, where he perceived that it was right and reasonable to do the corresponding, consequential actions.

58

(At this point let me say briefly, in parenthesis, that the word "Karma" has come to Europe by way of the English language, and because of its spelling people very often say "Karma" (with broad "ah" sound.) This is incorrect. It should be pronounced "Kärma" (with modified vowel sound.) I have always pronounced the word in this way and I regret that as a result many people have become accustomed to using the dreadful word "Kirma". For some time now you will have heard even very sincere students saying "Kirma." It is dreadful).

Thus, neither before nor after Initiation Science is there a contradiction between karmic necessity and freedom.

Once more, then: neither before nor after the entry of Initiation Science is there a contradiction between necessity—karmic necessity—and freedom. Before it there is none, because with everyday consciousness man remains within the realm of freedom, while karmic necessity goes on outside this realm, like any process of Nature. There is nothing in him to feel differently from what his own nature impels. Nor is there any contradiction after the entry of Initiation Science, for he is then quite in agreement with his karma, he thinks it only sensible to act according to it. Just as when you have built yourself a house and it is ready after a year, you do not say: the fact that you must now move in is an encroachment on your freedom. You will more probably say: Yes, on the whole it was quite sensible to build yourself a house in this neighbourhood and on this site. Now see to it that you are free in the house! Likewise he who looks back with Initiate-knowledge into his former lives on earth: he knows that he will become free precisely by the fulfilling of his karmic task—moving into the house which he built for himself in former lives on earth.

Thus, my dear friends, I wanted to explain to you the true compatibility of freedom and karmic necessity in human life. To-morrow we shall continue, entering more into the details of karma.

59

IV

To-day I wish to bring before you certain broader aspects concerning the development of karma, for we shall presently enter more and more into those matters which can only be illustrated—shall we say—by particular assumptions.

To gain a true insight into the progress of karma we must be able to imagine how man gathers his whole organisation together when he descends out of the spiritual world into the physical. You will understand that in the language of to-day there are no suitable forms of expression for these events which are practically unknown to our present civilisation. Therefore the terms we employ cannot but be inexact. When we descend out of the spiritual into the physical world, for a new life on earth, we have our physical body prepared for us, to begin with, by the stream of inheritance. This physical body is none the less connected in a certain sense, as we shall see, with the experiences we undergo between death and a new birth. To-day, however, it will suffice us to bear in mind that the physical body is given to us from the earthly side, whereas those members which we may describe as the higher members of the human being—the ether-body, astral body and Ego—come down out of the spiritual world.

Take first the ether-body. Man draws it together from the whole universal ether, before he unites himself with the physical body which is given to him by heredity. The union of the soul-spiritual man as Ego, astral body, and ether-body, with the physical human embryo, can only take place inasmuch as the ether-body of the mother-organism gradually withdraws itself from the physical embryo.

Man therefore unites himself with the physical germ after having drawn together his ether-body from the universal ether. The more precise description of these events will occupy us at a later stage. For the moment we are mainly interested

61

in the general question, whence come the several members which the human being has in earthly life between birth and death ? The physical organism comes, as we have seen, from the stream of inheritance, and the ether-organism from the universal ether from which it is first drawn together. As to the astral organism, we may truly say that the human being remains in all respects unconscious of it, or only subconsciously aware of it, during his earthly life. This astral body contains all the results of his life between death and a new birth. For between death and a new birth—according to what he has become through his preceding lives on earth, man enters into manifold relations with other human souls who are in the life between death and a new birth, and also with the spiritual Beings of a higher cosmic order who do not descend to earth in a human body, but have their being in the spiritual world.

All that a man brings over from his former lives on earth— precisely according to how he was and what he did—meets with the sympathy or antipathy of the beings whom he learns to know during his passage through the world between death and a new birth.

Not only is it of great significance for karma, what sympathies and antipathies he meets among the higher Beings according to the things he did in his preceding earthly life. Not only so; it is also of deep significance that he now comes into relation to those human souls to whom he was related on the earth, and there takes place a wonderful " reflection " as between his being and the being of the souls to whom on earth he was related. Let us assume he had a good relation to a soul whom he now meets again between death and a new birth. All that the good relationship implies, was living in him during his former life, or lives on earth; and this good relationship will now be mirrored in the other soul when he encounters him between death and a new birth.

Yes, it is really so. As he goes through the life between death and a new birth, man sees himself reflected everywhere in the souls with whom he is now living, because in effect he was living with them on the earth. If he did good to another human being, something is mirrored to him from the other's soul. If he did evil, something is mirrored likewise. ... And he now has the feeling—if I may use the word " feeling " with the reservations I made at the beginning—he has the feeling: " This human soul, you helped. All you experienced in helping him, all that you felt for this soul, the feelings that led you on to act thus helpfully towards him, your own inner experiences during the deed that helped him, are coming back to you now from his soul." Yes, they are actually mirrored to you from the other's soul.

Or again, you did harm to a human soul. That which was living in you while you did him harm, is mirrored back. And so you have your former earthly lives (and notably your last life) before you as though in a far and wide-spread reflector, mirrored by the souls with whom you were together.

Especially with respect to your life of action, you have the impression that it is receding from you. Between death and a new birth you lose the Ego-feeling—the sense of " I "— which was yours when in the body on earth. Indeed, you have lost it long ago. But you now get the feeling of " I " from this far-spread reflection. You come to life in the mirroring of your deeds, in the souls with whom you were during your earthly life.

On earth, your " I," your Ego, was in the body—as it were, a point. Between death and a new birth, it is mirrored to you from the surrounding circumference. This life is an intimate being-together with the other human souls— according to the relations you have entered into with them.

And this is a reality in the spiritual world. When we go through a room hung with many mirrors, we see ourselves reflected in each one. But—in ordinary human parlance— we know that the reflections are " not there." They do not remain when we go away; we are reflected no longer. But that which is reflected here in human souls remains; stays in existence. And there comes a time in the last third of the life between death and a new birth when we form our astral body out of these mirrored pictures. We draw all this into our astral body. In deed and truth, when we descend from

63

the spiritual world into the physical, we carry in our astral body what we have re-absorbed into ourselves, according to the way our actions of the former life on earth were mirrored in other souls between death and a new birth. This gives us the impulses which impel us towards or away from the human souls with whom we are born again in the physical body.

In this way the impulse to karma in a new earthly life is formed between death and a new birth—though I shall have to describe it more in detail in the near future; for we must take the Ego also into account.

Now we can trace how an impulse from one life works on into other lives. Take, for example, the impulse of love. We can do our deeds, in relation to other men, out of the impulse which we call love. It makes a great difference whether we do them out of a mere sense of duty, convention, respectability and so on, or whether we do them out of a greater or lesser degree of love.

Assume that in one earthly life a man is able to perform actions sustained by love, warmed through and through by love. It remains as a real force in his soul. What he takes with him as an outcome of his deeds, what is now mirrored in the other souls, comes back to him as a reflected image. And as he forms from this his astral body, with which he descends on to the earth, the love of the former earthly life, the love which he poured out and which was now returned to him from other souls, is changed to joy and gladness.

Such is the metamorphosis—if so we may describe it. A man does something for his fellow-men, something sustained by love. Love pouring out from him accompanies the actions which help his fellow-men. In the passage through life between death and a new birth, this outpouring love of the one life on earth is transmuted, metamorphosed, into joy that streams in towards him.

If you experience joy through a human being in one earthly life, you may be sure it is the outcome of the love you unfolded towards him in a former life. This joy flows back again into your soul during your life on earth. You know

64

the inner warmth which comes with joy, you know what joy can mean to one in life—especially that joy which comes from other human beings. It warms life and sustains it—as it were, gives it wings. It is the karmic result of love that has been expended.

But in our joy we again experience a relation to the human being who gives us joy. Thus, in our former life on earth, we had something within us that made the love flow out from us. In our succeeding life, already we have the outcome of it, the warmth of joy, which we experience inwardly once more. And this again flows out from us. A man who can experience joy in life, is again something for his fellow-men—something that warms them. He who has cause to go through life without joy is different to his fellow-men from one to whom it is granted to go through life with joyfulness.

Then, in the life between death and a new birth once more, what we thus experienced in joy between birth and death is reflected again in the many souls with whom we were on earth and with whom we are again in yonder life. And the manifold reflected image which thus comes back to us from the souls of those we knew on earth, works back again once more. We carry it into our astral body when we come down again into the next life on earth—that is the third in succession. Once more it is instilled, imprinted into our astral body. What is it in its outcome now? Now it becomes the underlying basis, the impulse for a quick and ready understanding of man and the world. It becomes the basis for that attunement of the soul which bears us along inasmuch as we have understanding of the world. If we find interest and take delight in the conduct of other men, if we understand their conduct and find it interesting in a given earthly life, it is a sure indication of the joy in our last incarnation and of the love in our incarnation before that. Men who go through the world with a free mind and an open sense, letting the world flow into them, so that they understand it well—they have attained through love and joy this relation to the world.

What we do in our deeds out of love is altogether different from what we do out of a dry and rigid sense of duty. You

65

will remember that I have always emphasised in my books: it is the deeds that spring from love which we must recognise as truly ethical; they are the truly moral deeds. How often have I indicated the great contrast in this regard, as between Kant and Schiller. Kant, both in life and in knowledge, " kantified " everything (" *Kante*," in German, means a hard edge or angle.—Note by translator.) In science, through Kant, all became hard and angular; and so it is in human action. " Duty, thou great and sublime name, thou who containest nothing of comfort or ease . . ."—this passage I quoted in my *Philosophy of Spiritual Activity* to the pretended anger (not the sincere, but the pretended, hypocritical anger) of many opponents, while over against it I set what I must establish as my view: " Love, thou who speakest with warmth to the soul. . . ."

Over against the dry and rigid Kantian concept of duty Schiller himself found the words: " *Gern dien' ich dem Freunde, doch tue ich es leider mit Neigung, drum wurmt es mich oft, dass ich nicht tugenhaft bin.*" (Gladly I serve my friends, yet alas, I do it with pleasure, wherefore it oftentimes gnaws me, I am not virtuous.) For in the Kantian ethic, that is not virtuous which we do out of real inclination, but only that which we do out of the rigid concept of duty.

Well, there are human beings who, to begin with, do not attain to love. Because they cannot tell their fellow-man the truth out of love (for if you love a man, you will tell him the truth, and not lies), because they cannot love, they tell the truth out of a sense of duty. Because they cannot love, out of a sense of duty they refrain from thrashing their fellow-man or from boxing his ears or otherwise offending him, the moment he does a thing they do not like. There is indeed a difference between acting out of a rigid sense of duty— necessary as it is in social life, necessary for many things— there is all the difference between this and the deeds of love.

Now the deeds that are done out of a rigid concept of duty, or by convention or propriety, do not call forth joy in the next life on earth. They too undergo that mirroring in other souls of which I spoke before; and, having done so, in the next life on earth they call forth what we may thus describe: " You feel that people are more or less indifferent to you." How many a person carries this through life. He is a matter of indifference to others, and he suffers from it. Rightly he suffers from it, for men are there for one another; man is dependent on not being a matter of indifference to his fellows. What he thus suffers is simply the outcome of a lack of love in a former life on earth, when he behaved as a decent man because of rigid duty hanging over him like a sword of Damocles. I will not say a sword of steel; that would be disquieting, no doubt, for most dutiful people; so let us say, a wooden sword of Damocles.

Now then, we are in the second earthly life.

That which proceeds as joy from love, in the third life becomes as we have seen, a free and open heart, bringing the world near to us, giving us open-minded insight into all things beautiful and good and true. While as to that which comes to us as the indifference of other men—what we experience in this way in one earthly life, will make us in the next life (that is, in the third) a person who does not know what to do with himself. Such a person, already in school, has no particular use for the things the teachers are doing with him. Then, when he grows a little older, he does not know what to become—mechanic or Privy Councillor, or whatever it may be. He does not know what to do with his life; he drifts through life without direction. In observation of the outer world, he is not exactly dull. Music, for instance —he understands it well enough, but it gives him no pleasure. After all, it is a matter of indifference whether the music is more or less good, or bad. He feels the beauty of a painting or other work of art; but there is always something in his soul that vexes: " What is the good of it anyhow ? What's it all for ? " Such are the things that emerge in the third earthly life in karmic sequence.

Now let us assume, on the other hand, that a man does positive harm to another, out of hatred or antipathy. We can imagine every conceivable degree. A man may harm his fellows out of a positively criminal sense of hatred. Or—to

67

omit the intermediate stages—he may merely be a critic. To be a critic, you must always hate a little—unless you are one who praises; and such critics are few nowadays. It is uninteresting to show recognition of other people's work; it only becomes interesting when you can be witty at their expense.

Now there are all manner of intermediate stages. But it is a matter here of all those human deeds which proceed from a cold antipathy—antipathy of which people are often not at all clearly aware—or, at the other extreme, from positive hatred. All that is thus brought about by men against their fellows, or against sub-human creatures—all this finds vent in conditions of soul which in their turn are mirrored in the life between death and a new birth. Then, in the next earthly life, out of the hatred is born what comes to us from the outer world as pain, distress, unhappiness caused from outside—in a word, the opposite of joy.

You will reply: we experience so much of suffering and pain; is it all really due to hatred—greater or lesser hatred—in our preceding life ? " I cannot possibly imagine," man will be prone to say, " that I was such a bad lot, that I must experience so much sorrow because I hated so much." Well, if you want to think open-mindedly of these things, you must be aware how great is the illusion which lulls you to sleep (and to which you therefore readily give yourself up) at this point. You suggest-away from your conscious mind the antipathies you are feeling against others. People go through the world with far more hatred than they think—far more antipathy, at least. It is a fact of life: hatred gives satisfaction to the soul, and for this reason, as a rule, it is not at first experienced in consciousness. It is eclipsed by the satisfaction it gives. But when it returns as pain and suffering that comes to us from outside, it is no longer so; we notice the suffering quickly enough.

Well, my dear friends, to picture, if I may, in homely and familiar fashion, the possibilities there are in this respect, think of an afternoon-tea, a real, genuine, gossiping party where half-a-dozen (half-a-dozen is quite enough) aunts or uncles—yes, uncles, too—are sitting together expatiating on their fellows. Think of it. How many antipathies are given vent to, what volumes of antipathy are poured out over other men and women, say in the course of an hour and a half—sometimes it lasts longer. In pouring out the antipathy they do not notice it; but when it comes back in the next earthly life, they notice it soon enough. And it does come back, inexorably.

Thus, in effect, a portion (not all, for we shall still learn to know other karmic connections) a portion of what we experience as suffering that comes to us from outside in one earthly life, may very well be due to our own feelings of antipathy in former lives on earth.

But with all this, we must never forget that karma—whatsoever karmic stream it may be—must always begin somewhere. If these are a succession of earthly lives:

a b c (d) e f g h

and this one, (d), is the present life, it does not follow that *all* pain which comes to us from without, is due to our former life on earth. It may also be an original sorrow, the karma of which will work itself out only in the next life on earth. Therefore I say, a *part*—even a considerable part—of the suffering that comes to us from outside is a result of the hatred we conceived in former lives.

And now, as we go on again into the third life, the outcome of the suffering which came to us (though only of that suffering which came, as it were, out of our own stored-up hatred), the outcome of the pain which was thus spent in our soul is a kind of mental dullness—dullness as compared with quick, open-minded insight into the world.

There may be a man who meets the world with a phlegmatic indifference. He does not confront the things of the world, or other men with an open heart. The fact is, very often, that he acquired this obtuseness of spirit by his sufferings in a former life on earth, the cause of which lay in his own karma. For the suffering which subsequently finds expression in this way, in dullness of soul, is sure to have been the result of feelings of hatred, at least in the last earthly life but one. You can be absolutely sure of it: stupidity in any one life is always the outcome of hatred in this or that preceding life. Yet, my dear friends, the true concept of karma must not only be based on this; it is not only to enable us to understand life. No, we must also conceive it as an impulse in life. We must be conscious that there is not only an a b c d, but an e f g h. That is to say, there are the coming earthly lives and what we develop as the content of our soul in this life will have its outcome and effect in the next life. If anyone wants to be extra stupid in his next earthly life but one, he need only hate very much in this life. But the converse is also true: if he wants to have free and open insight in the next earthly life but one, he need only love extra much in this life.

The insight into and knowledge of karma only gains real value when it flows into our will for the future, plays its part in our will for the future. And the moment has now come in human evolution when the unconscious cannot go on working as it did when our souls were passing through their former lives on earth. Men are becoming increasingly free and conscious. Since the first third of the 15th century we are in the age when men are becoming ever more free and conscious. And so for those men who are men of the present time, a next earthly life will already contain a dim feeling of preceding lives on earth. A man of to-day, if it occurs to him that he is not very bright, does not ascribe it to himself, but to his native limitations; following the current theories of materialism, he will generally ascribe it to his physical nature. Not so the men who return as the reincarnation of those of to-day. They will already possess at least a dim, disquieting feeling: if they are not very bright, somewhere or other there must have been something connected with feelings of antipathy or hatred.

And, if we now speak of a Waldorf School educational method, naturally for the present we must take account of the prevailing earthly civilisation. We cannot yet educate frankly towards a consciousness of life in terms of reincarnation, so to speak. For the people of to-day have not yet a feeling—

70

not even a dim feeling—of their repeated earthly lives. Nevertheless, the beginnings that have been made with the Waldorf School method will go on developing, if they are truly received. They will develop in the coming centuries, in this direction. This principle will be consciously applied in moral education. If a child has little talent, if a child is dull, it is somehow due to former lives in which he developed much hatred. With the help of spiritual science, you will try to find against whom the hatred may have been directed. For the men and women who were hated then, against whom the deeds inspired by hatred were done, must be there again somewhere or other in the child's environment. Education in coming centuries will have to be placed far more definitely into life. When you see what is coming to expression in such a child, in the metamorphosis of unintelligence in this life, you will then have to recognise from what quarters it is mirrored or rather *was* mirrored in the life between death and new birth. Then you will do something as educator so that this child will develop an especial love towards those for whom he felt specific hatred in former lives on earth. You will soon see the beneficial result of a love thus specifically roused and directed. The child's intelligence, nay, the whole life of his soul, will brighten.

It is not the general theories about karma which will help us in education, but this concrete way of looking into life, to see where the karmic connections lie. You will soon notice it; after all, the fact that destiny has brought these children together in one class is not a mere matter of indifference. People will get beyond the hideous carelessness that prevails in these things nowadays, when the " human material "—for so they often call it—which is thrown together in a class, is actually conceived as though it were bundled together by mere chance; not as though destiny had brought these human beings together. People will get beyond this appalling indifference. Then they will gain a new outlook as educators; they will be able to perceive the wonderful karmic threads that are woven between the one child and the other, as a result of their former lives.

71

Then they will bring consciously into the children's development that which can create a balance. For karma is, in a certain sense, inexorable. Out of an iron necessity we may write down the unquestioned sequence:

Love—Joy—an open heart.
Antipathy or Hatred—Suffering—Stupidity.

These are necessary connections. Nevertheless, we also stand face to face with a necessity when we see a river run its course; yet rivers have been regulated, their course has been known to be altered.

So likewise it is possible, as it were, to regulate the karmic stream, to work into it, to affect its course. Yes, it is possible.

If therefore in childhood you notice there is a tendency to dullness and stupidity and you perceive the connections, if now you guide the child to develop love in its heart, if you discover (which would be possible already to-day for people with a delicate observation of life), if you discover which are the other children to whom the child is karmically related, and you now bring the child to love them especially, to do deeds of love towards these other children—then you will give, to the antipathy that was, a counter-weight in the love: and in a next earthly life the dullness will have been improved.

There are educators, trained, as it were, by their own instinct who often do these things instinctively. Instinctively they will bring dull-witted children to the point where they develop love, thus educating them by degrees into more intelligent and perceptive beings.

It is only when we come to these things that our insight into the karmic connections becomes of real service to life.

Before we go on to pursue the detailed questions of karma, one other general question will naturally come before our souls. What sort of person is it—generally speaking—whom you may confront so as to know that you are karmically related to one another ? I must reply with a word which is sometimes used in a rather off-hand way nowadays: such a person is a " contemporary "; he is with us simultaneously on the earth.

Bearing this in mind, you will say to yourself: If you are with certain human beings in a life on earth, then you were with them in a former life (generally speaking, at least; there may of course, be displacements). And you were with them again in a life before it.

Now what of those who live fifty years later than you? They again were with other human beings in their former lives on earth. As a general rule, according to this line of thought, the human beings of the B series—shall I call it— will not come together with human beings of the A series.

It is an oppressive thought, but it is true. I shall afterwards speak of other doubts and questions, such as arise, for instance, when people say—as they so often do—" Humanity goes on increasing and increasing on the earth," and other things of that kind. To-day, however, I want to put this thought before you; perhaps it is an oppressive thought, but it is none the less true. It is a fact that the continued life of mankind on earth takes place in rhythms. One shift of human beings—if I may put it so—goes on, as a general rule, from one life to the next; so does another shift, and they are in a certain sense separated from one another. They do not find their way together in the earthly life, but only in the long intervening life between death and a new birth. There, indeed, they find their way together, but not in the earthly life. We come down again and again with a limited circle of people. Precisely from the point of view of reincarnation, to be contemporaries is a thing of inner importance, inner significance.

Why is it so? I can assure you, on the basis of spiritual

73

science, this question, which may well occupy one intellectually to begin with, has caused me the greatest imaginable pain. For it is necessary to bring out the truth, the inner nature of the fact. Thus you may ask: Why was I not a contemporary of Goethe's? Not having been a contemporary of Goethe's in this life, generally speaking—according to these truths—you can more or less conclude that you have never lived with him on earth. Goethe belongs to another shift.

What lies behind this? You must reverse the question; but to do so, you must have a real feeling, a perception of what the life of men together really is. You must be able to ask yourself a question on which I shall have very much to say in the near future: What is it really to be another man's contemporary? What is it, on the other hand, only to be able to know of him from history, as far as earthly life is concerned? What is it like?

We must indeed have a free mind, a sensitive heart, to answer these intimate questions: What is it like—with all the accompanying inner experiences of the soul—when a contemporary man is speaking to you, or doing any actions that come near you? What is it like? And having gained the necessary perception of this, you must then be able to compare it with what it would be like if you encountered a person who is not your contemporary, and probably has never been so in any life on earth, whom you may none the less revere—more, perhaps, than any of your contemporaries. What would it be like if you met him as a contemporary? In a word—forgive the personal note—what would it be like if I were a contemporary of Goethe? If you are not an insensitive, indifferent kind of person. . . . Needless to say, if you are insensitive and have no feeling for what a contemporary can be, you are scarcely in a position to answer such a question. What would it be like if I, walking down the Schillergasse, let us say, towards the Frauenplan in Weimar, had suddenly encountered " the fat Privy Councillor," say in the year 1826 or 1827? One knows quite well, one could not have borne it. You can stand your contemporary; you

74

cannot bear a man who, in the nature of the case, cannot be your contemporary. In a sense, he acts like a poison on your inner life. You can only bear him inasmuch as he is not your contemporary, but your predecessor or successor.

Of course, if you have no feeling for such things, they remain in the unconscious; but you can well imagine a man who has an intimate feeling for spiritual things . . . if he knew that as he went down the Schillergasse towards the Frauenplan in Weimar, he would encounter the " fat Privy Councillor "—Goethe, with the double chin—he would feel himself inwardly impossible. A man who has no feeling for such things—he no doubt would just have taken off his hat!

These things are not to be explained out of the earthly life. The reasons why we cannot be contemporary with a man are in fact, not contained within the earthly life. To see them, we must penetrate into the spiritual facts. Therefore, for earthly life, such things appear paradoxical. Nevertheless, they are as I have said.

I can assure you, with genuine love I wrote the introduction to Jean Paul's works, published in the *Cotta'sche Bibliothek der Weltliteratur*. Yet, if I had ever had to sit side by side with Jean Paul at Bayreuth, it would have given me a stomach-ache, without doubt! That does not hinder one's having the highest reverence. And it is so for every human being—only with most people it remains in the sub-conscious, in the astral or in the ether-body; it does not affect the physical. The experience of the soul which affects the physical body must also become conscious.

You must be well aware of this, my dear friends. If you want to gain knowledge of the spiritual world, you cannot escape hearing of things which will seem grotesque and paradoxical. The spiritual world is different from the physical. Of course, it is easy enough for anyone to turn to ridicule the statement that if I had been a contemporary of Jean Paul's, it would have given me a stomach-ache to have to sit beside him. That is quite true—it goes without saying for the everyday, banal, Philistine world of earthly life. But the laws of the banal and Philistine world do not determine the spiritual facts. You must accustom yourselves to think in other forms of thought, if you wish to understand the spiritual world; you must be prepared to experience many surprising things. When the everyday consciousness reads about Goethe, it may naturally feel impelled to say: " How I should like to have known him personally, to have shaken him by the hand! " and so on. It is a piece of thoughtlessness; for there are laws according to which we are predestined for a given epoch of the earth. In this epoch we can live. It is just as in our physical body we are predestined for a certain pressure of air; we cannot rise above the earth to a height where the pressure no longer suits us. Nor can a man who is destined for the 20th century live in the time of Goethe.

These were the things I wanted to bring forward about karma, to begin with.

V

Speaking in detail about karma, we must of course distinguish between those karmic events of life which come to a man more from outside, and those which arise, as it were, from within. A human being's destiny is composed of many and diverse factors. To begin with, it depends on his physical and etheric constitution. Then it depends on the sympathies and antipathies with which he is able to meet the outer world, according to his astral and his Ego-constitution; and on the sympathies and antipathies with which others in their turn are able to encounter him according to his nature. Moreover, it depends on the myriad complications and entanglements in which he finds himself involved on the path of life. All these things work together to determine—for a given moment, or for his life as a whole—the human being's karmic situation.

I shall now try to show how the total destiny of man is put together from these several factors. To-day we shall take our start from certain inner factors in his nature. Let us observe, for once, what is in many respects of cardinal importance. I mean, his predisposition to health and illness; and, with this underlying basis, all that comes to expression in his life, in the physical strength—and strength of soul—with which he is able to confront his tasks, and so on. . . .

To judge these factors rightly, we must however be able to see beyond many a prejudice that is contained in the civilisation of to-day. We must be able to enter more into the true original being of man; we must gain insight, what it really signifies to say that man, as to his deeper being, descends from spiritual worlds into this physical and earthly life.

All that people refer to nowadays as heredity, has even found its way, as you are well aware, into the realms of poetry and art. If any one appears in the world with such and such qualities, people will always begin by asking how he inherited them. If, for example, he appears with a predisposition to illness, they will at once ask, what of the hereditary circumstances ?

To begin with, the question is quite justifiable; but in their whole attitude to these things nowadays, people look past the real human being; they completely miss him. They do not observe what his true being is, how his true being unfolds. In the first place, they say, he is the child of his parents and the descendant of his forebears. Already in his physiognomy, and even more perhaps in his gestures, they fondly recognise a likeness to his ancestors emerging. Not only so; they see his whole physical organism as a product of what is given to him by his forefathers. He carries this physical organism with him. They emphasise this very strongly, but they fail to observe the following:

When he is born, to begin with undoubtedly man has his physical organism from his parents. But what is the physical organism which he receives from his parents ? The thoughts of the civilisation of to-day upon this question are fundamentally in error. For in effect, when he is at the change of teeth, man not only exchanges the teeth he first received, for others, but this is also the moment in life when the entire human being—as organisation—is for the first time renewed. There is a thorough-going difference as between what the human being becomes in his eighth or ninth year of life, and what he was in his third or fourth year. It is a thorough-going difference. That which he was—as organisation—in his third or fourth year, that he undoubtedly received by heredity. His parents gave it to him. That which emerges first in the eighth or ninth year of his life is in the highest degree a product of what he himself has brought down from spiritual worlds.

To picture the real underlying facts, we may put it as follows—though I am well aware it will shock the man of to-day. Man, we must say, when he is born, receives something like a model of his human form. He gets this model from his forefathers; they give him the model to take with

78

him into life. Then, working on the model, he himself develops what he afterwards becomes. What he develops, however, is the outcome of what he himself brings with him from the spiritual world.

Fantastic as it may seem to the man of to-day—to those who are completely immersed in modern culture—yet it is so. The first teeth which the human being receives are undoubtedly inherited; they are the products of heredity. They only serve him as the model, after which he elaborates his second teeth, and this he does according to the forces he brings with him from the spiritual world. Thus he elaborates his second teeth. And as it is with the teeth, so with the body as a whole.

A question may here arise: Why do we human beings need a model at all? Why can we not do as indeed we did in earlier phases of earth-evolution? Just as we descend and gather in our ether-body (which, as you know, we do with our own forces, and bring it with us from the spiritual world), why can we not likewise gather to ourselves the physical materials and form our own physical body without the help of physical inheritance?

For the modern man's way of thinking, it is no doubt an grotesquely foolish question—mad, I need hardly say. But with respect to madness—let us admit it—the Theory of Relativity holds good. To begin with, people only apply the Theory to movements. They say you cannot tell, from observation, whether you yourself—with the body on which you are—are moving, or whether it is the neighbouring body that is moving. This fact emerged very clearly when the old cosmic theory was exchanged for the Copernican. Though, as I said, they apply the Theory of Relativity only to movements, yet we may also apply it (for it certainly has its sphere of validity) to the aforesaid " madness." Here are two people, standing side by side: each one is mad as compared to the other. . . . The question only remains, which of the two is absolutely mad?

In relation to the real facts of the spiritual world, this question must none the less be raised: Why does the human being need a model? Ancient world-conceptions answered it in their way. Only in modern time, when morality is no longer included in the cosmic order but only recognised as human convention, these questions therefore are no longer asked. Ancient world-conceptions not only asked the question; they also answered it. Originally, they said, man was pre-destined to come to the earth in such a way that he could form his own physical body from the substances of earth, just as he gathers to himself his ether-body from the cosmic ether-substance. But he then fell a prey to the Luciferic and Ahrimanic influences, and he thereby lost the faculty, out of his own nature to build his physical body. Therefore he must take it from heredity. This way of obtaining the physical body is the result of inherited sin.

This is what ancient world-conceptions said—that this is the fundamental meaning of "inherited sin." It signifies the having to enter into the laws and conditions of heredity.

We in our time must first discover and collect the necessary concepts so as to take these questions sincerely, in the first place; and in the second place, to find the answers. It is quite true: man in his earthly evolution has not remained as strong as he was pre-disposed to be before the onset of the Luciferic and Ahrimanic influences. Therefore he cannot form his physical body of his own accord when he comes down into the earthly conditions. He is dependent on the model, he needs the model which we see growing in the first seven years of human life. And, as he takes his direction from the model, it is but natural if more or less of the model also remains about him in his later life. If, in his working on himself, he is altogether dependent on the model, then he forgets—if I may put it so—what he himself brought with him. He takes his cue entirely from the model. Another human being, having stronger inner forces as a result of former lives on earth, takes his direction less from the model; and you will see how greatly such a human being changes in the second phase of life, between the change of teeth and puberty.

This is precisely the task of school. If it is a true school, it should bring to unfoldment in the human being what he has brought with him from spiritual worlds into this physical life on earth.

Thus, what the human being afterwards takes with him into life will contain more or less of inherited characteristics, according to the extent to which he can or cannot overcome them.

Now all things have their spiritual aspect. The body man has in the first seven years of life is simply the model from which he takes his direction. Either his spiritual forces are to some extent submerged in what is pressed upon him by the model; then he remains quite dependent on the model. Or else, in the first seven years, that which is striving to change the model works its way through successfully.

This striving also finds expression outwardly. It is not merely a question of man's working on the model. While he is doing so, the original model gradually loosens itself, peels off, so to speak—falls away. It all falls away, just as the first teeth fall away. Throughout this process, the forms and forces of the model are pressing on the one hand, while on the other hand the human being is trying to impress what he himself has brought with him to the earth. . . . There is a real conflict in the first seven years of life. Seen from the spiritual standpoint, this conflict is signified by that which finds expression—outwardly, symptomatically—in the illnesses of childhood. The typical diseases of childhood are an expression of this inward struggle.

Needless to say, similar forms of illness often occur later in life. In such a case—to take only one example—it may be that the patient did not succeed very well in overcoming the model in the first seven years of life. And at a later age an inner impulse arises, after all to rid himself of what has thus karmically remained in him. Thus in the 28th or 29th year of life, a human being may suddenly feel inwardly roused, all the more vigorously to beat against the model, and as a result, he or she will get some illness of childhood.

If you have an eye for it, you will soon see how remarkable it is in some children—how greatly they change in physiog-

81

nomy or gesture after the 7th or 8th year of their life. Nobody knows where the change comes from. The prevailing views of heredity are so strong nowadays that they have passed into the everyday forms of speech. When, in the 8th or 9th year, some feature suddenly emerges in the child (which, in real fact, is deeply, organically rooted) the father will often say: " Anyhow, he hasn't got it from me." To which the mother will answer: " Well, certainly not from me." All this is only due to the prevailing belief which has found its way into the parental consciousness—I mean of course, the belief that the children must have got everything from their parents.

On the other hand, you may often observe how children grow even more like their parents in this second phase of life than they were before. That is quite true. But we must take in earnest what we know of the way man descends into the physical world.

Among the many dreadful flowers of the swamp which psycho-analysis has produced, there is the theory of which you can read on all hands nowadays, namely that in the hidden sub-conscious mind every son is in love with his mother and every daughter with her father; and they tell of the many conflicts of life which are supposed to arise from this, in the sub-conscious regions of the soul. All these are of course amateurish interpretations of life. The truth however is, that the human being is in love with his parents already before he comes down into earthly life. He comes down just because he likes them.

Of course, the judgment of life which people have on earth must differ in this respect from the judgment they have outside the earthly life between death and a new birth. On one occasion, in the early stages of our anthroposophical work, a lady appeared among us who said: " No," when she heard of reincarnation. She liked the rest of Anthroposophy very well, but with reincarnation she would have nothing to do; one earthly life, she said, was quite enough for her. Now we had very well-meaning followers in those days, and they tried in every imaginable way to convince the good lady that the idea was true after all, that every human being must undergo repeated lives on earth. She could not be moved. One friend belaboured her from the left, and another from the right. After a time, she left; but two days later, she wrote me a post-card to the effect that, after all, she was not going to be born again on earth!

To such a person, one who wishes simply to tell the truth from spiritual knowledge can only say: No doubt, while you are here on earth, it is not at all to your liking that you should come down again for a future life. But it does not depend on that. Here on earth, to begin with, you will go through the gate of death into the spiritual world. That you are quite willing to do. Whether or no you want to come down again will depend on the judgment which will be yours when you no longer have the body about you. For you will then form quite a different judgment.

The judgments man has in physical life on earth are, in fact, different from the judgments he has between death and a new birth. For there the point of view is changed. And so it is, if you say to a human being here on earth—a young human being, perhaps—that he has chosen his father, it is not out of the question that he might make objection: " Do you mean to say that I have chosen the father who has given me so many thrashings ? " Yes, certainly he has chosen him; for he had quite another point of view before he came down to earth. He had the point of view that the thrashings would do him a lot of good. . . . Truly, it is no laughing matter; I mean it in deep earnestness.

In the same way, man also chooses his parents as to form and figure. He himself has a picture before him—the picture that he will become like them. He does not become like them by heredity, but by his own inner forces of soul-and-spirit—the forces he brings with him from the spiritual world. Therefore you need to judge in an all-round way out of both spiritual and physical science. If you do so, it will become utterly impossible to judge as people do when they say, with the air of making an objection: " I have seen children who became all the more like their parents in their second phase of life." No doubt; but then the fact is, that these children

83

themselves have set themselves the ideal of taking on the form of their parents.

Man really works, throughout the time between death and a new birth, in union with other departed souls, and with the beings of the Higher Worlds; he works upon what will then make it possible for him to build his body.

You see, we very much under-estimate the importance of what man has in his sub-consciousness. As earthly man, he is far wiser in the sub-conscious than in the surface-consciousness. It is indeed out of a far reaching, universal, cosmic wisdom that he elaborates within the model that afterwards emerges in the second phase of life—what he then bears as his own human being, the human form that properly belongs to him. In time to come, people will know how little they really receive—as far as the substance of the body is concerned—from the food they eat. Man receives far more from the air and the light, from all that he absorbs in a very finely-divided state from air and light, and so on. When this is realised, people will more readily believe that man builds up his second body quite independently of any inherited conditions. For he builds it entirely from his world-environment. The first body is actually only a model and that which comes from the parents—not only substantially, but as regards the outer bodily forces—is no longer there in the second period of life. The child's relation to his parents then becomes an ethical, a soul-relationship. Only in the first period of life—that is until the seventh year—is it a physical, hereditary relationship.

Now there are human beings who, in this earthly life, take a keen interest in all that surrounds them in the visible cosmos. They observe the world of plants, of animals; they take interest in this thing and that in the visible world around them. They take an interest in the majestic picture of the star-lit sky. They are awake, so to speak, with their soul, in the entire physical cosmos. The inner life of a human being who has this warm interest in the cosmos differs from the inner life of one who goes past the world with a phlegmatic, indifferent soul.

In this respect, the whole scale of human characters is represented. There, for example, is a man who has been quite a short journey. When you afterwards talk to him, he will describe with infinite love the town where he has been, down to the tiniest detail. Through his keen interest, you yourself will get a complete picture of what it was like in the town he visited.

From this extreme we can pass to the opposite. On one occasion, for instance, I met two elderly ladies; they had just travelled from Vienna to Pressburg, which is a beautiful city. I asked them what it was like in Pressburg, what had pleased them there. They could tell me nothing except that they had seen two pretty little dachshunds down by the river-side! Well, they need not have gone to Pressburg to see the dachshunds; they might just as well have seen them in Vienna. However, they had seen nothing else at all.

So do some people go through the world. And, as you know, between these outermost ends of the scale, there are those who take every kind and degree of interest in the physical world around them.

Suppose a man has little interest in the physical world around him. Perhaps he just manages to interest himself in the things that immediately concern his bodily life—whether, for instance, one can eat more or less well in this or that district. Beyond that, his interests do not go; his soul remains poor. He does not imprint the world into himself. He carries very little in his inner life, very little of what has radiated into him from the phenomena of the world, through the gate of death into the spiritual realms. Thereby he finds the working with the spiritual beings, with whom he is then together, very difficult. And as a consequence, in the next life he does not bring with him, for the up-building of his physical body, strength and energy of soul, but weakness—a kind of faintness of soul. The model works into him strongly enough. The conflict with the model finds expression in manifold illnesses of childhood; but the weakness persists. He forms, so to speak, a frail or sickly body, prone to all manner of illnesses. Thus, karmically, our interest of soul-and-spirit in the one earthly life is transformed into our constitution as to health in the next life. Human beings who are " bursting with health " certainly had a keen interest in the visible world in a former incarnation. The detailed facts of life work very strongly in this respect.

No doubt it is more or less " risqué " nowadays to speak of these things, but you will only understand the inner connections of karma if you are ready to learn about the karmic details. Thus, for example, in the age when the human souls who are here to-day were living in a former life on earth, there was already an art of painting; and there were some human beings even then who had no interest in it at all. Even to-day, you will admit, there are people who do not care whether they have some atrocity hanging on the walls of their room, or a picture beautifully painted. And there were also such people in the time when the souls who are here to-day were living in their former lives on earth. Now, I can assure you, I have never found a man or a woman with a pleasant face— a sympathetic expression—who did not take delight in beautiful paintings in a former life on earth. The people with an unsympathetic expression (which, after all, also plays its part in karma, and signifies something for destiny) were always the ones who passed by the works of art of painting with obtuse and phlegmatic indifference.

These things go even farther. There are human beings (and so there were in former epochs of the earth) who never look up to the stars their whole life long, who do not know where Leo is, or Aries or Taurus; they have no interest in anything in this connection. Such people are born, in a next life on earth, with a body that is somehow limp and flabby. Or if, by the vigour of their parents, they get a model that carries them over this, they become limp, lacking in energy and vigour, through the body which they then build for themselves.

And so it is with the entire constitution which a man bears with him in a given life on earth. In every detail we might refer it to the interests he had in the visible world—in an all-embracing sense—in his preceding life on earth.

86

People, for instance, who in our time take absolutely no interest in music—people to whom music is a matter of indifference—will certainly be born again in a next life on earth either with asthmatic trouble, or with some disease of the lung. At any rate, they will be born with a tendency to asthma or lung disease. And so it is in all respects; the quality of soul which develops in our earthly life through the interest we take in the visible world, comes to expression in our next life in the general tone of our bodily health or illness.

Here again, some one might say: To know of such things may well take away one's taste for a next life on earth. That again, is judged from the earthly standpoint, which is certainly not the only possible standpoint; for, after all, the life between death and a new birth lasts far longer than the earthly life. If a man is obtuse and indifferent with regard to anything in his visible environment, he takes with him an inability to work in certain realms between death and a new birth. He passes through the gate of death with the consequences of his lack of interest. After death he goes on his way. He cannot get near certain Beings; certain Beings hold themselves away from him; he cannot get near them. Other human souls with whom he was on earth, remain as strangers to him. This would go on for ever, like an eternal punishment of Hell, if it could not be modified. The only cure, the only compensation, lies in his resolving—between death and a new birth—to come down again into earthly life and experience in the sick body what his inability has signified in the spiritual world. Between death and a new birth he longs for this cure, for he is then filled with the consciousness that there is something he cannot do. Moreover, he feels it in such a way that in the further course, when he dies once again and passes through the time between death and new birth, that which was pain on earth becomes the impulse and power to enter into what he missed last time.

Thus we may truly say: in all essentials, man carries health and illness with him with his karma, from the spiritual world into the physical. Of course we must bear in mind that it is not always a fulfilment of karma, for there is also karma in process of becoming. Therefore we shall not relate to his former life on earth, everything the human being has to suffer in his physical life as regards health and illness. None the less we may know: in all essentials, that which emerges— notably from within outward—with respect to health and illness, is karmically determined as I have just described.

Here again, the world becomes intelligible only when we can look beyond this earthly life. In no other way can we explain it; the world cannot be explained out of the earthly life.

If we now pass from the inner conditions of karma which follow from a man's organisation, to the more outward aspect, here once again—only to strike the chords of karma, so to speak—we may take our start from a realm of facts which touches man very closely. Take, for example, our relation to other human beings, which is psychologically very much connected with the conditions of our health and illness, at any rate as regards the general mood and attunement of our soul.

Assume, for example, that someone finds a close friend in his youth. An intimate friendship arises between them; the two are devoted to one another. Afterwards life takes them apart—both of them, perhaps, or one especially—they look back with a certain sadness on their friendship in youth. But they cannot renew it. However often they meet in life, their friendship of youth does not arise again. How very much in destiny can sometimes depend on broken friendships of youth. You will admit, after all, a person's destiny can be profoundly influenced by a broken friendship of youth.

Now one investigates the matter. . . . I may add that one should speak as little as possible about these things out of mere theory. To speak out of theory is of very little value. In fact, you should only speak of such things either out of direct spiritual perception, or on the basis of what you have heard or read of the communications of those who are able to have direct spiritual vision, provided you yourselves find the communications convincing, and understand them well. There is no value in theorising about these things. Therefore

I say, when you endeavour with spiritual vision to get behind such an event as a broken friendship of youth, as you go back into a former life on earth, this is what you generally find. The two people, who in a subsequent earthly life, had a friendship in their youth which was afterwards broken—in an earlier incarnation they were friends in later life.

Let us assume, for instance: two young people—boys or girls—are friends until their twentieth year. Then the friendship of their youth is broken. Go back with spiritual cognition into a former life on earth, and you will find that again they were friends. This time, however, it was a friendship that began about the twentieth year and continued into their later life. It is a very interesting case, and you will often find it so when you pursue things with spiritual science.

Examine such cases more closely and to begin with, this is what you find: If you enjoyed a friendship with a person in the later years of life, you have an inner impulse also to learn to know what he may be like in youth. The impulse leads you in a later life actually to learn to know him as a friend in youth. In a former incarnation you knew him in maturer years. This brought the impulse into your soul to learn to know him now also in youth. You could no longer do so in that life, therefore you do it in the next.

It has a great influence when this impulse arises—in one of the two or in both of them—and passes through death and lives itself out in the spiritual world between death and a new birth. For in the spiritual world, in such a case, there is something like a " staring fixedly " at the period of youth. You have an especial longing to fix your gaze on the time of youth, and you do not develop the impulse to learn to know your friend once more in maturer years. And so, in your next life on earth, the friendship of youth—pre-determined between you by the life you lived through before you came down to earth—is broken.

This is a case out of real life, for what I am now relating is absolutely real. One question, however, here arises: What was the older friendship like in the former life, what was it like, that rouses the impulse in you to have your friend with you only in *youth* in a new life on earth ? The answer is this: for the desire to have the other being beside you in your youth and yet not to develop into a desire to keep him as your intimate friend in later life as well, something else must also have occurred. In all the instances of which I am aware, it has invariably been so: If the two human beings had remained united in their later life, if their friendship of youth had not been broken they would have grown tired and bored with one another: because, in effect, their friendship in maturer years in a former life took a too selfish direction. The selfishness of friendships in one earthly life avenges itself karmically in the loss of the same friendships in other lives.

These things are complicated indeed; but you can always get a guiding line if you see this, for it is so in many cases: Two human beings go their way, each of them apart, say, till their twentieth year; thenceforward they go along in

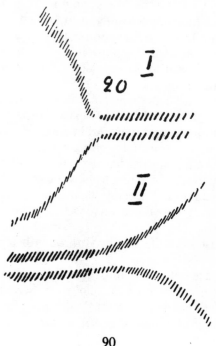

friendship (I). Then in the next earthly life, correspondingly, we generally get this second picture (II)—the picture of friendship in youth, after which their lives go apart.

This too you will find very often: If, in your middle period of life in one incarnation, you meet a human being who has a strong influence on your destiny (these things, of course, only hold good as a general rule—not in all cases), it is very likely that you had him beside you by forces of destiny at the beginning and at the end of your life in a previous incarnation. Then the picture is so: In the one incarnation you live through the beginning and ending of life together; in the other incarnation you are not with him at the beginning or at the end, but you encounter him in the middle period of life.

Or again it may be that in your childhood you are united by destiny with another human being; in a former life you were united with him precisely in the time before you approached your death. Such inverse reflections often occur in the relationships of karma.

VI

If we now continue our studies of karma, it is necessary for us in the first place to perceive how karma enters into man's development. We must perceive, that is to say, how destiny, interwoven as it is with the free deeds of man, is really shaped and moulded in its physical reflection out of the spiritual world.

To begin with, I shall have to say a few things concerning the human being as he lives on earth. During these lectures we have been studying earthly man in relation to the various members of his being. We have distinguished in him the physical body, the etheric body, the astral body and the organisation of the Ego. But there is yet another way of perceiving his several members, namely when we direct our gaze upon him, simply as he stands before us in the physical world.

In to-day's lecture—independently of what we have already been discussing—we shall therefore approach a different distinction of the members of the human being. Then we shall try to build a bridge between what we discuss to-day and that which is already known to us.

Observing the human being as he stands before us on the earth—simply according to his physical form—we can recognise in this physical form and configuration three clearly distinct members. If they are not generally distinguished, it is only because that which counts as science nowadays looks at the facts in a merely superficial way. It has no feeling for what reveals itself when these things are observed with a perception that is illumined from within. There, to begin with, is the head of man. Even outwardly considered, we can perceive that this human head appears quite different from the remainder of the human form. We need but observe the origin of man out of the embryo. The first thing we can see developing as human embryo is the head organisation. That is practically all that we can see to begin with. The whole human organisation takes its start from the head. All that afterwards flows into man's form and figure and configuration, is, in the embryo, a mere system of appendages. As physical form, man to begin with is head, and head alone. The other organs are there as mere appendages. In the first period of embryo existence, the functions these organs assume in later life—as breathing, circulation, nutrition and so on—are not undertaken as such from within the embryo. The corresponding functions are supplied from without inward, so to speak: provided for by the mother-organism, through organs that afterwards fall away—organs that are no longer attached to the human being later on.

Man, to begin with, is simply a head. He is altogether "head," and the remaining organs are only appendages. It is no exaggeration to say that man, to begin with, is a head. The remainder is merely an appendage. Then, at a later stage, the organs which to begin with were mere appendages, grow and gain in importance. Therefore, in later life, the head is not strictly distinguished from the rest of the body. But that is only a superficial characterisation of the human being. For in reality, even as physical form, he is a threefold being. All that constitutes his original form—namely the head—remains throughout his earthly life as a more or less individual member. People only fail to recognise the fact, but it is so.

You will say: Surely one ought not to divide the human being in this way—beheading him, so to speak, chopping his head off from the rest of his body. That such is the anthroposophical practice was only the fond belief of the Professor, who reproached us for dividing man into head-, chest-organs and limb-organs. But it is not so at all. The fact is rather this: that which appears outwardly as the formation of the head is only the main expression of the human head-formation. Man remains "head" throughout his whole earthly life. The most important sense-organs, it is true—the eyes and ears, the organs of smell and organs of taste—are in the actual head. But the sense of warmth, for example, the sense of pressure, the sense of touch, are spread over the whole human being. That is precisely because the three members cannot in fact be separated spatially. They can at most be separated in the sense that the head-formative principle is mainly apparent in the outward form of the head, while in reality it permeates the whole human being. And so it is too, for the other members. The " head " is also there in the big toe throughout man's earthly life, inasmuch as the big toe possesses a sense of touch or a sense of warmth.

Thus we have characterised, to begin with, the one member of the human being as he stands before us in the sense-world. In my books I have also described this one organisation as the system of nerves and senses; for that is to characterise it more inwardly. This, then, is the one member of the human being, the organisation of nerves and senses. The second member is all that lives and finds expression in rhythmical activity. You cannot say of the nerves-and-senses system that it finds expression in rhythmic activity. For if it did, in the perception of the eye, for instance, you would have to perceive one thing at one moment and then another, and a third and a fourth; and then return again to the first, and so on. In other words, there would have to be a rhythm in your sense-perceptions; and it is not so. Observe on the other hand the main features of your chest-organisation. There you will find the rhythm of the breathing, the rhythm of circulation, the rhythm of digestion and so forth. . . . There, everything is rhythmical.

This rhythm, with the corresponding organs of rhythm, is the second thing to develop in the human being; and it extends once more over the whole human being, though its chief external manifestation is in the organs of the chest. The whole human being is heart, is lung; yet lung and heart are localised, so to speak, in the organs, so-called. It is well known that the whole human being breathes; you breathe at every place in your organism. People speak of a skin-breathing. Only here, once more, the breathing function is mainly concentrated in the activity of the lung.

The third thing in man is the limb-organism. The limbs

come to an end in the trunk or chest-organism. In the embryo-stage of existence they appear as mere appendages. They are the latest to develop. They however are the organs mainly concerned in our metabolism. For by their movement—and inasmuch as they do most of the work in the human being—the metabolic process finds its chief stimulus.

Therewith we have characterised the three members that appear to us in the human form. But these three members are intimately connected with the soul-life of man. The life of the human soul falls into Thinking, Feeling and Willing. Thinking finds its corresponding physical organisation chiefly in the organisation of the head. It has its physical organisation, it is true, throughout the human being; but that is only because the head itself, as I said just now, is there throughout the human being.

Feeling is connected with the rhythmic organisation. It is a prejudice—even a superstition on the part of modern science to suppose that the nervous system has anything directly to do with feeling. The nervous system has nothing directly to do with feeling at all. The true organs of feeling are the rhythms of the breathing, of the circulation. . . . All that the nerves do is to enable us to form the concept that we have our feelings. Feelings, once more, have their own proper organisation in the rhythmic organism. But we should know nothing of our feelings if the nerves did not provide for our having ideas about them. Because the nerves provide us with the ideas of our own feelings, modern intellectualism conceives the superstitious notion that the nerves themselves are the organs of our feeling. That is not the case.

But when we consciously observe our feelings—such as they arise out of our rhythmic organism—and compare them with the thoughts which are bound to our head, our nerves-and-senses organisation, then, if we have the faculty to observe such things at all, we perceive just the same difference between our thoughts and our feelings as between the thoughts which we have in our day-waking life, and our dreams. Our feelings have no greater intensity in consciousness than dreams. They only have a different form; they only make

96

their appearance in a different way. When you dream in pictures, your consciousness is living in the pictures of the dream. These pictures, however, in their picture-form, have the same significance as in another form our feelings have. Thus we may say: We have the clearest and most light-filled consciousness in our ideas and thoughts. We have a kind of dream-consciousness in our feelings. We only imagine that we have a clear consciousness of our feelings; in reality we have no clearer consciousness of our feelings than of our dreams. When, on awaking from sleep, we recollect ourselves and form wide-awake ideas about our dreams, we do not by any means catch at the actual dream. The dream is far richer in content than what we afterwards conceive of it. Likewise is the world of feeling infinitely richer than the ideas, the mental pictures of it, which we make present to our conscious mind.

And when we come to our willing—that is completely immersed in sleep. Willing is bound to the limbs—and metabolic and motor organism. All that we really know of our willing are the thoughts. I form the idea: I will pick up this watch.

Think of it quite sincerely, and you will have to admit: You form the idea: " I will take hold of the watch." Then you take hold of it. As to what takes place, starting from the idea and going right down into the muscles, until at length you have an idea once more (namely, that you are actually taking hold of the watch) following on your original idea— all this that goes on in your bodily nature between the mental picture of the intention and the mental picture of its realisation, remains utterly unconscious. So much so that you can only compare it with the unconsciousness of deep, dreamless sleep.

We do at least dream of our feelings, but of our impulses of will we have no more than we have from our sleep.

You may say: I have nothing at all from sleep. Needless to say, we are not speaking from the physical standpoint; from a physical standpoint it would of course be absurd to say that you had nothing from sleep. But in your soul too, in reality, you have a great deal from your sleep. If you never slept, you would never rise to the Ego-consciousness.

 *now*

Here it is necessary to realise the following. When you remember the experiences you have had, you go backward—as along this line (see diagram). Beginning from now, you go backward. You generally imagine that it is so—that you go farther and farther backward along the line. But it is not so at all. In reality you only go back until the last time you awakened from sleep. Before that moment you were sleeping. All that lies in this intervening part of the line (see diagram) is blotted out; then from the last time you fell asleep until the last time but one when you awakened, memory follows once more. So it goes on. In reality, as you look back along the line, you must always interpose the periods of unconsciousness. For a whole third of our life, we must insert unconsciousness. We do not observe this fact. But it is just as though you had a white surface, with a

black hole in the centre of it. You see the black hole, in spite of the fact that none of the forces are there. Likewise it is when you remember. Although no reminiscences of life are there (for the intervals of sleep), nevertheless you see the black nothingness—that is, the nights you have slept through.

98

Your consciousness impinges on them every time, and that is what really makes you call yourself: " I." If it went on and on, and nowhere impinged on anything, you would never rise to a consciousness of " I."

Thus we can certainly say that we have something from sleep. And just as we have something from our sleep in the ordinary sense of earthly life, so do we have something from that sleep which always prevails in our willing. We pass asleep through that which is really going on in us in every act of will. And just as we get our Ego-consciousness from the black void in this case (referring to the diagram), so likewise our Ego is inherent in that which is sleeping in us during the act of will. It is, however, that Ego which goes throughout our former lives on earth.

That is where karma holds sway, my dear friends. Karma holds sway in our willing. Therein are working and wielding all the impulses from our preceding life on earth; only they too, even in waking life, are veiled in sleep.

Once more, therefore: when we conceive man as he stands before us in earthly life, he appears to us in a threefold form: the head-organisation, the rhythmic and the motor-organisation. The three are diagrammatically divided here, but we will always bear in mind that each of the members belongs in its turn to the whole man. Moreover, Thought is bound to the head-organisation, Feeling to the rhythmic organisation, Willing to the motor-organisation. Wide awake consciousness is the condition in which our ideas, our mental presentations, are. Dreaming is the condition in which our feelings are. Deep sleep (even in waking life) is the condition in which our volition is. We are asleep in our impulses of will, even in waking life.

Now we must learn to distinguish two things about the head, that is, about our life of ideation. We must divide the head, so to speak, more intimately. We shall thus be led to distinguish between what we have as momentary ideas or mental pictures in our intercourse with the world and what we have as memory. As you go about in the world, you are constantly forming ideas according to the impressions you receive. But it also remains possible for you subsequently to draw the ideas forth again out of your memory. Moreover, the ideas you form in your intercourse with the world in the given moment are not inherently different from the ideas that are kindled in you when memory comes into play. The difference is that in the one case they come from outside, and in the other from within.

It is indeed a naïve conception to imagine that memory works in this way: that I now confront a thing or event, and form an idea or mental presentation of it; that the idea goes down into me somewhere or other, as if into some cupboard or chest, and that when I afterwards remember it, I fetch it out again. Why, there are whole philosophies describing how the ideas go down beneath the threshold of consciousness, to be fished out again in the act of recollection. These theories are utterly naïve. There is of course no such chest where the ideas are lying in wait. Nor is there anywhere in us where they are moving about, or whence they might walk out again into our head, when we remember them. All these things are utterly non-existent, nor is there any explanation in their favour. The fact is rather as follows:

You need only think of this. When you want to memorise something, you generally work not merely with the activity of forming ideas. You help yourself by quite other means. I have sometimes seen people in the act of memorising; they formed ideas, they thought as little as possible. They performed outward movements of speech—pretty vehement movements, repeated again and again, like this (with the arms), " *und es wallet und woget und brauset und zischt* " (a line of Schiller's poem: *The Diver*). Many people memorise in this way, and in so doing, they think as little as possible. And to add a further stimulus, they sometimes hammer the forehead with their fist. That, too, is not unknown.

The fact is that the ideas we form as we go about the world are evanescent, like dreams. It is not the ideas which have gone down into us, but something quite different that emerges out of our memory. To give you an idea of it, I should have to draw it thus—

100

Of course it is only a kind of symbolic diagram. Imagine the human being in the act of sight. He sees something. (I will not describe the process in any greater detail; we might do so, but for the moment we do not need it.) He sees something. It goes in through his eye, through the optic nerve into the organs into which the optic nerve then merges.

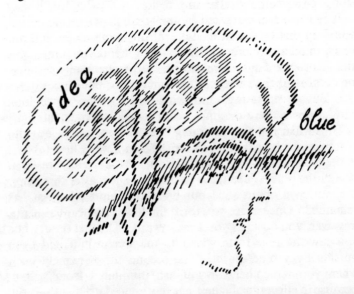

We have two clearly distinct members of our brain—the more outer peripheric brain, the grey matter; and beneath it, the white matter. Then the white matter merges into the sense-organs. Here is the grey matter (see the diagram); it is far less evolved than the white. The terms " grey " and " white " are, of course, only approximate. Thus, even crudely, anatomically considered it is so: The objects make an impression on us, passing through the eye and on into the processes that take place in the white matter of the brain. Our ideas or mental presentations, on the other hand, have their organ in the grey matter, which, incidentally, has quite a different cell-structure, and there the ideas are lighting up and vanishing like dreams. There the ideas are flickering up, because beneath this region (compare the diagram once more) the process of the impressions is taking place.

If it depended on the ideas going down into you somewhere, and you then had to fetch them out again in memory, you would remember nothing at all. You would have no memory. It is really like this: In the present moment, let us say, I see something. The impression of it (whatever it may be) goes into me, mediated by the white matter of the brain. The grey matter works in its turn, dreaming of the impressions, making pictures of them. The mental pictures come and go; they are quite evanescent. As to what really remains, we do not conceive it at all in this moment, but it goes down into our organisation, and when we remember, we look within; down there the impression remains permanent.

Thus when you see something blue, an impression goes into you from the blue (below, in the diagram), while here (above, in the diagram) you yourself form an idea, a mental presentation of the blue. The idea is transient. Then, after three days perhaps, you observe in your brain the impression that has remained. Once more you form the idea of blue. This time, however, you do so as you look inward. The first time, when you saw the blue from without, you were stimulated from outside by a blue object. The second time—namely now, when you remember it—you are stimulated from within, because in effect the blueness has reproduced itself within you. In both cases it is the same process, namely a process of perception. Memory too is perception. In effect, our day-waking consciousness consists in ideation, in the forming of ideas; but there—beneath the ideation—certain processes are going on. They too, rise into our consciousness by an act of ideation, namely by our forming of ideas in the act of memory. Underneath this activity of ideation is the perceiving, the pure process of perception. And, underneath this in turn, is Feeling.

Thus we can distinguish more intimately, in our head-organisation or thought-organisation—the perceiving and the activity of ideation. What we have perceived, we can then remember. But it actually remains very largely unconscious; it is only in memory that it rises into consciousness. What really takes place in man is no longer experienced in consciousness by man himself. When he perceives, he experiences in consciousness the idea, the mental presentation of it. The real effect of the perception goes into him. Out of this real effect, he is then able to awaken the memory. But at this place the unconscious already begins.

In reality it is only here, in this region (see the diagram)—where, in our waking-day consciousness we form ideas—it is only here that we ourselves are, as Man. Only here do we really have ourselves as Man. Where we do not reach down with our consciousness (for we do not even reach to the causes of our memories), where we do not reach down, there we do not have ourselves as Man, but are incorporated in the world.

It is just as it is in the physical life—you breathe in; the air you now have in yourself was outside you a short while ago, it was the-air-of-the-world; now it is your air. After a short time you give it back again to the world. You are one with the world. The air is now outside you, now within you. You would not be Man at all, if you were not so united with the world as to have not only that which is within your skin, but that with which you are connected in the whole surrounding atmosphere. And as you are thus connected on the physical side, so it is as to your spiritual part: the moment you get down into the next subconscious region—the region out of which memory arises—you are connected with that which we call the Third Hierarchy: Angeloi, Archangeloi, Archai. Just as you are connected through your breathing with the air, so are you connected with the Third Hierarchy through your head-organisation, namely the lower head-organisation. This, which is only covered over by the outermost lobes of the brain, belongs solely to the earth. What is immediately beneath is connected with the Third Hierarchy: Angeloi, Archangeloi, Archai.

Now let us go down into the region, psychologically speaking, of feeling: corporeally speaking, of the rhythmic organisation, out of which the dreams of our Feeling life arise. There, less than ever do we have ourselves as Man. There we are connected with what constitutes the Second Hierarchy—spiritual Beings who do not incarnate in any earthly body, for they remain in the spiritual world. But they are continually sending their currents, their impulses, the forces that go out from them, into the rhythmic organisation of man. Exusiai, Dynamis, Kyriotetes—they are the Beings whom we bear within our breast.

Just as we bear our own human Ego actually only in the outermost lobes of the brain, so do we bear the Angeloi, Archangeloi, etc. immediately beneath this region; yet still within the organisation of the head. There is the scene of their activities on earth; there are the starting-points of their activity. And in our breast we carry the Second Hierarchy—Exusiai and the rest. In our breast are the starting points of their activity.

And as we now go down into our motor-organism, the organism of movement, in this the Beings of the First Hierarchy are active: Seraphim, Cherubim and Thrones.

The transmuted food-stuffs, the food-stuffs we have eaten, circulate in our limbs. There in our limbs, they undergo a process. It is really a living process of combustion. For if we take only a single step, there arises in us a living process of combustion, a burning-up of that which is, or was, outside us. We ourselves, as Man, are connected with this combustion process. As physical human beings with our limbs and metabolic-organism, we are connected with the lowest. And yet it is precisely through the limb-organisation that we are connected with the highest. With the First Hierarchy—Seraphim, Cherubim, and Thrones—we are connected by virtue of what imbues us there with spirit.

Now the great question arises (it may sound trivial when I clothe it in earthly words, but I can do no other), the question arises: What are they doing—these Beings of the three successive Hierarchies, who are in us—what are they doing?

The answer is: the Third Hierarchy, Angeloi, Archangeloi, etc.—concern themselves with that which has its physical organisation in the human head, i.e. with our thinking. If they were not concerning themselves with our thinking—with that which is going on in our head—we should have no memory in ordinary earthly life. For it is the Beings of this Hierarchy who preserve in us the impulses which we receive with our perceptions. They are underlying the activity which reveals itself in our memory; they lead us through our earthly life in this first sub-conscious, or unconscious, region.

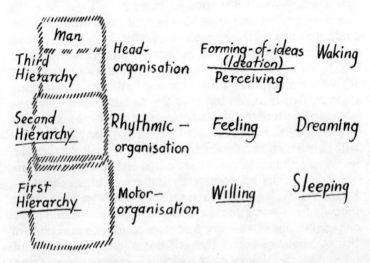

Now let us go on to the Beings of the Second Hierarchy—Exusiai, etc. They are the Beings we encounter when we have passed through the gate of death, that is, in the life between death and a new birth. There we encounter the souls of the departed, who lived with us on earth; but we encounter, above all, the spiritual Beings of this Second Hierarchy—the Third Hierarchy together with them, it is true, but the Second Hierarchy are the most important there. With them we work in our time between death and a new birth—we work upon all that we felt in our earthly life, all that we brought about in our organisation. Thus, in union with these Beings of the Second Hierarchy, we elaborate our coming earthly life.

When we stand here on the earth, we have the feeling that the spiritual Beings of the Divine World are above us. When

105

we are in yonder sphere, between death and a new birth, we have the opposite idea—the Angeloi, Archangeloi, etc., who guide us through our earthly life, as above described, live, after our death, on the same level with us—so to speak. And immediately beneath us are the Beings of the Second Hierarchy. With them we work out the forming of our inner karma. All that I told you yesterday of the karma of health and illness—we work it out with these Beings, the Beings of the Second Hierarchy. And when, in that time between death and new birth, we look still further down—as it were, looking *through* the Beings of the Second Hierarchy—then we discover, far below, the Beings of the First Hierarchy, Cherubim, Seraphim, and Thrones.

As earthly man, we look for the highest Gods above us. As man between death and a new birth, we look for the highest Divinity (attainable for us human beings, to begin with) in the farthest depths beneath us. We, all the time, are working with the Beings of the Second Hierarchy, elaborating our inner karma between death and a new birth: that inner karma which afterwards comes forth, imaged in the health or illness of our next life on earth. While we ourselves are engaged in this work—working alone, and with other human beings, upon the bodies that will come forth in our next life on earth—the Beings of the First Hierarchy are active far below us, and in a strange way. That one beholds. For with respect to their activity—a portion, a small portion of their activity—they are actually involved in a Necessity. They, as the creators of the earthly realm, are obliged to follow and reproduce what the human being has fashioned and done during his life on earth. They are obliged to reproduce it—though in a peculiar way.

Think of a man in his earthly life: in his Willing (which belongs to the First Hierarchy), he accomplishes certain deeds. The deeds are good or evil, wise or foolish. The Beings of the First Hierarchy—Seraphim, Cherubim, Thrones—are under necessity to form and mould the counter-images thereto in their own sphere.

You see, my dear friends, we live together. Whether the

106

things we do with one another are good or evil; for all that is good, for all that is evil, the Beings of the First Hierarchy must shape the corresponding counterparts. Among the First Hierarchy, all things are judged; yet not only judged, but shaped and fashioned. Thus between death and a new birth, while we ourselves are working at our inner karma with the Second Hierarchy and with other departed souls, meanwhile we behold what Seraphim, and Cherubim and Thrones have experienced through our deeds on earth.

Yes, here upon earth the blue vault of the sky arches over us, with its cloud-forms and sunshine and so forth; and in the night, the star-lit sky. Between death and a new birth the living activity of Seraphim, Cherubim and Thrones extends like a vault beneath us. And we gaze down upon them— Seraphim, Cherubim and Thrones—even as we here look up to the clouds, and the blue, and the star-strewn sky. Beneath us, there, we see the Heavens, formed of the activity of Seraphim, Cherubim and Thrones. But what kind of activity ? We behold among the Seraphim, Cherubim, Thrones, the activity which results as the just and compensating activity from our own deeds on earth—our own, and the deeds through which we lived with other men. The Gods themselves are obliged to carry out the compensating action, and we behold them as our Heavens, only the Heavens are there beneath us. In the deeds of the Gods we see and recognise the consequences of our earthly deeds—whether this deed or that be good or evil, wise or foolish. And, as we thus look downward, between death and a new birth, we relate ourselves to the mirrored image of our deeds, just as in earthly life we relate ourselves to the vault of heaven above us.

As to our own inner karma, we ourselves bring it into our inner organism. We bring it with us on to the earth as our faculties and talents, our genius and our stupidity. Not so what the Gods are fashioning there beneath us; what they have to experience in consequence of our earthly lives comes to us in our next life on earth as the facts of Destiny which meet us from without. We may truly say, the very thing we pass through asleep carries us in our earthly life into our Fate. But in this is living what the corresponding Gods, those of the First Hierarchy, had to experience in their domain as the consequences of our deeds during the time between our death and a new birth.

One always feels a need to express these things in pictures. Suppose we are standing somewhere or other in the physical world. The sky is overcast; we see the clouded sky. Soon afterwards, fine rain begins to trickle down; the rain is falling. What hitherto was hovering above us, we see it now in the wet fields and the trees, sprinkled with fine rain. So it is when we look back with the eye of the Initiate, from human life on earth into the time we underwent, before we came down to this earth, that is to say, the time we underwent between our last death and our last birth. For there we see the forming of the deeds of the Gods in consequence of our own deeds in our last life on earth. And then we see it, spiritually raining down, so to become our destiny.

Do I meet a human being whose significance for me in this life enters essentially into my destiny? That which takes place in our meeting was lived in advance by the Gods as a result of what he and I had in common in a former earthly life. Am I transplanted during my earthly life into a district —or a vocation—which is important for me? All that approaches me there as outer destiny is the image of what was experienced by Gods—Gods of the First Hierarchy—in consequence of my former life on earth, during the time when I was myself between death and a new birth.

One who thinks abstractly will think: " There are the former lives on earth; the deeds of the former lives work across into the present. Then they were the causes, now they are the effects." But you cannot think far along these lines; you have little more than words when you enunciate this proposition. But behind what you thus describe as the Law of Karma, are deeds and experiences of the Gods; and only behind all that is the other. . . .

When we human beings confront our destiny only by way of feeling, then we look up, according to our faith, to the

108

Divine Beings or to some Providence on which we feel the course of our earthly life depends. But the Gods—namely those Gods whom we know as belonging to the First Hierarchy, Seraphim, Cherubim and Thrones—have, as it were, an inverse religious faith. They feel their Necessity among men on earth—men, whose creators they are. The aberrations human beings suffer, and the progressions they enjoy, must be balanced and compensated by the Gods. Whatever the Gods prepare for us as our destiny in a subsequent life, they have lived it before us.

These truths must be found again through Anthroposophy. Out of a consciousness not fully developed, they were perceived by mankind in a former, instinctive clairvoyance. The Ancient Wisdom did indeed contain such truths. Afterwards only a dim feeling remained of them. In many things that meet us in the spiritual history of mankind, the dim feeling of these things is still in evidence. You need but remember the verse by Angelus Silesius which you will also find quoted in my writings. To a narrow religious creed, it sounds impertinent:

I know that without me God can no moment live;
If I come to naught, He needs must give up the Ghost.*

Angelus Silesius went over to Roman Catholicism; it was as a Catholic that he wrote such verses. He was still aware that the Gods are dependent on the world, even as the world is dependent on them. He knew that the dependence is mutual; and that the Gods must direct their life according to the life of men. But the Divine Life works creatively, and works itself out in turn in the destinies of men. Angelus Silesius, dimly feeling the truth, though he knew it not in its exactitude, exclaimed:

I know that without me God can no moment live;
If I come to naught, He needs must give up the Ghost.

*From *The Cherubinic Wanderer*. Book I. 8.

The Universe and the Divine depend on one another, and work into one another. To-day we have recognised this living interdependence in the example of human destiny or karma.

VII

In the last lecture I spoke of how the forces of karma take shape, and to-day I want to lay the foundations for acquiring an understanding of karma through studying examples of individual destinies. Such destinies can only be illustrations, but if we take our start from particular examples we shall begin to perceive how karma works in human life. It works, of course, in as many different ways as there are human beings on the earth, for the configuration of karma is entirely individual. And so whenever we turn our attention to a particular case, it must be regarded merely as an example.

To-day I shall bring forward examples I have myself investigated and where the course of karma has become clear to me. It is of course a hazardous undertaking to speak of individual karmic connections, no matter how remote the examples may be, for in referring to karma it has become customary to use expressions of everyday language such as: " This is caused by so-and-so; this or that blow of destiny must be due to such and such a cause, how the man came to deserve it " . . . and so forth. But karma is by no means as simple as that, and a great deal of utterly trivial talk goes on, particularly on this subject!

To-day we will consider certain examples of the working of karma, remote though they may be from our immediate life. We will embark upon the hazardous undertaking of speaking about the karma of individuals—as far as my investigations make this possible. I am therefore giving you examples which are to be taken as such.

I want to speak, first, of a well-known aestheticist and philosopher, *Friedrich Theodor Vischer*. I have often alluded to him in lectures, but to-day I will bring into relief certain characteristic features of his life and personality which can provide the basis for a study of his karma.

111

Friedrich Theodor Vischer received his education at the time when German idealistic philosophy—particularly Hegelian thought—was in its heyday. Friedrich Theodor Vischer, a young man pursuing his studies among people whose minds were steeped in the Hegelian mode of thinking, adopted it himself. The absorption in transcendental thoughts that is characteristic of Hegel strongly appealed to Vischer. It was clear to him that, as Hegel asserts, thought is the Divine Essence of the universe, and that when we, as human beings, think, when we live in thoughts, we are living in the Divine Substance.

Friedrich Theodor Vischer was steeped in Hegelian philosophy. But he was a person who displayed in a very marked way the traits and characteristics of the folk from which he sprang. He had all the traits of a typical Swabian: he was obstinate, dogmatic, disputatious, exceedingly independent; his manner was abrupt, off-hand. He also had very striking personal peculiarities. To take his outward appearance first, he had beautiful blue eyes and a reddish-brown beard, which in spite of its scrubbiness he wore with a certain aesthetic enthusiasm! I say " aesthetic enthusiasm " because in his writings he minces no words about men who wear no beards, calling them " beardless monkey-faces "! As you see, his language is anything but restrained; all his remarks come out with the abrupt, off-handed assurance of a typical Swabian.

He was a man of medium height, not stout, in fact rather slight in build, but he walked the streets holding his arms as if he were forcing a way for himself with his elbows—which is an exact picture of what he did in a spiritual sense! So much for his outward appearance.

He had a passionately independent nature and would say just what he pleased, without any restraint whatever. It happened one day that he had been slandered by " friends " in the Stuttgart Council—such things are not unusual among friends!—and he was severely reprimanded by the Council. It chanced that on the very same day a little son was born to him—the Robert Vischer who also made a name for himself as an aestheticist—and the father announced the event in the lecture-hall with the words: " Gentlemen, to-day I have been given a big *Wischer* (wigging) and a little Vischer! "

It was characteristic of him to speak very radically about things as he found them. For example, he wrote an amusing article entitled: " On the Foot Pest in Trains." It enraged him to see people sitting in a railway carriage with their feet up on the opposite seat. He simply could not endure it and his article on the subject is really enchanting.

What he wrote in his book on fashions,* about the ill-breeding and lack of adequate clothing at dances and other entertainments, had better not be mentioned here. To put it briefly, he was a very original and forceful personality!

A friend of mine once paid him a visit, knocking politely at the door. I do not know whether it is a custom in Swabia, but Vischer did not say " Come in," or what is usually said on such occasions. He yelled out " *Glei* "—meaning that he would be ready immediately.

While still comparatively young, Vischer embarked on a weighty task, namely that of writing a work on aesthetics according to the principles of Hegelian philosophy. These five volumes are a truly remarkable achievement. You will find in them the strict division into paragraphs which was habitual with Hegel, and the characteristic definitions. If I were to read a passage to you, you would all yawn, for it is written in the anything but popular style of Hegel, all in abrupt definitions, such as: The Beautiful is the appearance of the Idea in material form. The Sublime is the appearance of the Idea in material form, but the Idea predominates over the material form. The Comic is the appearance of the Idea in material form, but the material form predominates over the Idea . . . and so on and so forth. These statements are certainly not without interest, but the book goes a great deal further. As well as the abrupt definitions, you have what is called the " small print," and most people when they are reading the book leave out the large print and read only the small—which as a matter of fact contains some of the very cleverest writing on aesthetics that is anywhere to be found.

*Mode und Zynismus. Stuttgart, 1878.

113

There is no pedantry, no Hegelian dialectic here; it is Vischer, the true Swabian, with all his meticulousness and at the same time his fine and delicate feeling for the beautiful, the great and the sublime. Here, too, you find Nature and her processes described in a way that defies comparison, with an exemplary freedom of style. Vischer worked at the book for many years, bringing it to its end with unfaltering consistency.

At the time when this work appeared, Hegelianism was still in vogue and appreciation was widespread. Needless to say, there were opponents, too, but on the whole the book was widely admired. In course of time, however, a vigorous opponent appeared on the scenes, a ruthless critic who pulled the book to pieces until not a shred of good was left; everything was criticised in a really masterly style. And this critic was none other than Friedrich Theodor Vischer himself in his later years! There is an extraordinary charm about this critique of himself in his *Kritische Gängen* (Paths of Criticism).

As aestheticist, philosopher and man of letters, Vischer published a wealth of material in *Kritische Gängen*, and subsequently in the fine collection of essays entitled *Altes und Neues* (Old and New). While still a student he wrote lyrics in an ironic vein. In spite of the great admiration I have always had for Vischer, I could never help being of opinion that the productions of his student days were not even student-like, but sheer philistinism. And this trait came out in him again in his seventies, when he wrote a collection of poems under the pseudonym "*Schartenmayer*." Here there is philistinism par excellence!

He was an out-and-out philistine in regard to Goethe's *Faust*. Part One . . . well, he admitted there was something good in it, but as for Part Two—he considered it a product of senility, so many fragments patched together. He maintained that it ought to have been quite different, and not only did he write his *Faust, der Tragödie dritter Teil*, in which he satirises Goethe's Part Two, but he actually drew up a plan of just how Goethe ought to have written *Faust*. That is philistinism and no mistake! It is almost on a par with what Du Bois-Reymond, the eminent scientist, said in his lecture " Goethe,

114

Nothing but Goethe." He said: " *Faust* is a failure. It would have been all right if Faust had not engaged in such tomfoolery as the invocation of spirits or the calling up of the Earth-Spirit, but had simply and straightforwardly invented an electrical machine or an air pump and restored to Gretchen her good name. . . ." And there is exactly the same kind of philistinism in what Vischer says about *Faust*.

Perhaps it would not be put like this in Württemberg, but in my homeland in Austria we should say that he gave Goethe's *Faust* a good " Swabian thrashing "! Such expressions differ slightly in meaning, of course, according to the districts where they are used.

It is these traits that are significant in Vischer. They really make up his personality. One might also, of course, give details of his life, but I do not propose to do that. My aim has been to give you a picture of his personality and with this as a foundation we can proceed to a study of his karma. To-day I wanted simply to give you the material for this study.

A second personality of whose karma I want to speak, is *Franz Schubert*, the composer. As I said, it is a daring venture to give particular examples in this way, but it is right that they should be given and to-day I shall lay the foundations.

Here too, I shall select the features that will be needed when we come to speak of Schubert's karma. Practically all his life he was poor. Some time after his death, however, many persons claiming to have been not only his acquaintances but his " friends " were to be found in Vienna! A whole crowd of people, according to themselves, had wanted to lend him money, spoke of him affectionately as " little Franz " and the like. But during his lifetime it had been a very different story!

Schubert had, however, found one real friend. This friend, Baron von Spaun, was an extraordinarily noble-minded man. He had cared for Schubert with great tenderness from the latter's earliest youth, when they were school-fellows, and he continued to do so in later years. In regard to karma it seems to me particularly significant—as we shall find when we come to consider the working of karma—that

Spaun was in a profession quite alien to his character. He was a highly cultured man, a lover of art in every form, and a close friend not only of Schubert but also of Moritz von Schwind. He was deeply sensitive to everything in the way of art. Many strange things happen in Austria—as you know, Grillparzer was a clerk in the fiscal service—and Spaun too, who had not the slightest taste for it, spent his whole life in Treasury offices. He was an official engaged in administering finance, dealing with figures all the time. When he reached a certain age he was appointed Director of Lotteries! He had charge of lotteries in Austria—a task that was most distasteful to him. But now just think what it is that a Director of Lotteries has to control. He has, so to speak, to deal at a high level with the passions, the hopes, the blighted expectations, the disappointments, the dreams and superstitions of countless human beings. Just think of what has to be taken into account by a Director of Lotteries—a Chief Director at that. True, you may go into his office and come out again without noticing anything very striking. But the reality is there nevertheless, and those who take the world and its affairs in earnest must certainly reckon with such things.

This man, who had no part whatever in the superstitions, the disappointments, the longings, the hopes, with which he had to deal—this man was the intimate friend of Schubert, deeply and intensely concerned for his material as well as his spiritual well-being. One can often be astounded, outwardly speaking, at what is possible in the world! There is a biography of Schubert in which it is said that he looked rather like a negro. There is not a grain of truth in it. He actually had a pleasing, attractive face. What *is* true, however, is that he was poor. More often than not, even his supper, which he was in the habit of taking in Spaun's company, was paid for with infinite tact by the latter. Schubert had not enough money even to hire a piano for his own use. In outward demeanour—Spaun gives a very faithful picture here—Schubert was grave and reserved, almost phlegmatic. But an inner, volcanic fire could at times burst from him in a most surprising way.

116

A very interesting fact is that the most beautiful motifs in Schubert's music were generally written down in the early morning; as soon as he had wakened from sleep he would sit down and commit his most beautiful motifs to paper. At such times Spaun was often with him, for as is customary among the intellectuals of Vienna, both Schubert and Spaun liked a good drink of an evening, and the hour was apt to get so late that Schubert, who lived some distance away, could not be allowed to go home but would spend the night on some makeshift bed at his friend's house. On such occasions Spaun was often an actual witness of how Schubert, on rising in the morning, would write down his beautiful motifs, as though they came straight out of sleep.

The rather calm and peaceful exterior did not betray the presence of the volcanic fire lying hidden in the depths of the soul. But it was there, and it is precisely this aspect of Schubert's personality that I must describe to you as a basis for the study of his karma.

Let me tell you what happened on one occasion. Schubert had been to the Opera. He heard Gluck's *Iphigenia* and was enraptured by it. He expressed his enthusiasm to his friend Spaun during and after the performance in impassioned words, but at the same time with restraint. His emotions were delicate and tender, not violent. (I am selecting the particular traits we shall need for our study.) The moment Schubert heard Gluck's *Iphigenia*, he recognised it as a masterpiece of musical art. He was enchanted with the singer Milder; and Vogl's singing so enraptured him that he said his one wish was to be introduced to him in order that he might pay homage at his feet. When the performance was over, Schubert and Spaun went to the so-called *Bürgerstubl* (Civic Club Room) in Vienna. I think they were accompanied by a third person whose name I have not in mind at the moment. They sat there quietly, although every now and again they spoke enthusiastically about their experience at the Opera. Sitting with others at a neighbouring table was a University professor well known in this circle. As he listened to the expressions of enthusiasm his face began to flush and became redder and redder. Then he began to mutter to himself, and when the muttering had gone on for a time without being commented on by the others, he fell into a rage and shouted across the table: " *Iphigenia*!—it isn't real music at all; it's trash. As for Milder, she hasn't an idea of how to sing, let alone bring off runs or trills! And Vogl—why he lumbers about the stage like an elephant! "

And now Schubert was simply not to be restrained! At any minute there was danger of a serious hand-to-hand scuffle. Schubert, who at other times was calm and composed, let loose his volcanic nature in full force and it was as much as the others could do to quieten him.

It is important for the life we are studying that here we have a man whose closest friend is a Treasury official, actually a Director of Lotteries, and that the two are led together by karma. Schubert's poverty is important in connection with his karma, because in these circumstances there was little opportunity for his anger to be roused in this way. Poverty restricted his social intercourse, and it was by no means often that he could have such a neighbour at table, or give vent to his volcanic nature.

If we can picture what was really happening on that occasion, and if we remember the characteristics of the people from whom Schubert sprang, we can ask ourselves the following question. (Negative supposition is of course meaningless in the long run, but it does sometimes help to make things clear.) We can ask ourselves: If the conditions had been different (of course they couldn't have been, only, as I say, the question can make for clarification)—if the conditions had been different, if Schubert had had no opportunity of giving expression to the musical talent within him, if he had not found a devoted friend in Spaun, might he not have become a mere brawler in some lower station in life? What expressed itself like a volcano that evening in the club room, was it not a fundamental trait in Schubert's character? Human life defies explanation until we can answer the question: How does the metamorphosis come about whereby in a certain life a man does not, so to say, live out his pugnacity

118

but becomes an exquisite musician, the pugnacity being transformed into subtle and delicate musical phantasy ?

It sounds paradoxical and grotesque, but for all that it is a question which, if we consider life in its wider range, must needs be asked, for it is only when we study such things that the deeper problems of karma really come into view.

The third personality of whom I want to speak is *Eugen Dühring*, a man much hated, but also—by a small circle—greatly loved. My investigations into karma have led me to occupy myself with this individual, too, and as before I will give you, first of all, the biographical material.

Eugen Dühring was a man of extraordinary gifts. In his youth he studied a whole number of subjects, particularly from the aspect of mathematics, including branches of knowledge such as political economy, philosophy, mechanics, physics and so on.

He gained his doctorate with an interesting treatise, and then in a book, long since out of print, followed up the same theme with great clarity and forcefulness. I will tell you a little about it. The subject is almost as difficult as the Theory of Relativity, but, after all, people have been talking about the Theory of Relativity for a long time now and, without understanding a single word, have considered, and still do consider it, quite wonderful. Difficult as the subject is, I want to tell you, in a way that will perhaps be comprehensible, something about the thoughts contained in this earliest work of Dühring.

The theme is as follows.—People generally picture to themselves: Out there is space, and it is infinite. Space is filled with matter. Matter is composed of minute particles, infinite in number. An infinite number of tiny particles have conglomerated into a ball in universal space, have in some way crystallised together, and the like. Then there is time, infinite time. The world has never had a beginning; neither can one say that it will have an end.

These vague, indefinite concepts of infinity were repellent to the young Dühring, and he spoke with great perspicacity when he said that all this talk about infinity is devoid of real meaning, that even if one has to speak of myriads and myriads of world-atoms, or world-molecules, there must nevertheless be a definite, calculable number. However vast universal space is conceived to be, its magnitude must be capable of computation; so too, the stretch of universal time. Dühring expounded this theme with great clarity.

There is something psychological behind this. Dühring's one aim was clarity of thought, and there is no clear thinking at all in these notions of infinity. He went on to apply his argument in other domains, for example to the so-called " negative quantities." Positive quantities (e.g. when something is possessed) are distinguished from negative quantities by writing a minus sign before the latter. Thus here you have 0 (zero), in one direction plus 1, and in the other direction minus 1, and so on.

Dühring maintains that all this talk about minus quantities is absolute nonsense. What does a " negative quantity," a " minus number " mean? He says: If I have 5 and take away 1, then I have 4; if I have 5 and take away 2, then I have 3; if I have 5 and take away 4, then I have 1; and if I have 5 and take away 5, then I have 0. The advocates of negative quantities say: If I have 5 and take away 6, then I have minus 1; if I have 5 and take away 7, then I have minus 2.

Dühring maintains that there is no clarity of thinking here. What does " minus 1 " mean? It means: I am supposed to take 6 from 5; but then I have 1 too little. What does " minus 2 " mean? I am supposed to take 7 from 5; but then I have 2 too little. What does " minus 3 " mean? I am supposed to take 8 from 5; but then I have 3 too little. There is no difference between the negative numbers, *as* numbers, and the positive numbers. The negative numbers mean only that when I have to subtract, I have too little by a particular amount. And Dühring went on to apply the same principle to mathematical concepts of many kinds.

I know how deeply I was impressed by this as a young man,

120

for Dühring brought real clarity of thought to bear upon these things.

He displayed the same astute discernment in the fields of national economy and the history of philosophy, and became a lecturer at the University of Berlin. His audiences were very large and he lectured on a variety of subjects: national economy, philosophy, mathematics.

It so happened that a prize was offered by the Academy of Science at Göttingen for the best book on the history of mechanics. It is usual in such competitions for the essays to be sent in anonymously. The competitor chooses a motto, his name is contained inside a closed envelope with the motto written outside, so that the adjudicators are unaware of the author's identity.

The Göttingen Academy of Science awarded the prize to Eugen Dühring's *History of Mechanics* and wrote him a most appreciative letter. Therefore Dühring was not only recognised by his own circle of listeners as an excellent lecturer, but now gained the recognition of a most eminently learned body.

Along with all the talents which will be evident to you from what I have been saying, this same Dühring had a really malicious tongue—one cannot call it anything else. There was something of the malicious critic about him in regard to everything in the world. As time went on he exercised less and less restraint in this respect; and when such an eminently learned body as the Göttingen Academy of Science awarded him the prize, it acted like a sting upon him. It was quite in the natural course of things, but nevertheless it stung. And then we see two qualities beginning to be combined in him: an intensely strong sense of justice—which he undoubtedly possessed—and on the other hand an extraordinary propensity for abuse.

Just at the time when he was stung into abuse and sarcasm, Dühring had the misfortune to lose his sight. In spite of total blindness, however, he continued to lecture in Berlin. He went on with his work as an author, and was always able, up to a point, of course, to look after his affairs himself.

About this time a truly tragic destiny in the academic world during the 19th century came to his knowledge—the destiny of Julius Robert Mayer, who was actually the discoverer of the heat-equivalent in mechanics and who, as can be stated with all certainty, had been shut up in an asylum through no fault of his own, put into a strait-jacket and treated shamefully by his family, his colleagues and his " friends." It was at this time that Dühring wrote his book, *Julius Robert Mayer, the Galileo of the 19th Century.* And it was in truth a kind of Galileo-destiny that befell Julius Robert Mayer.

Dühring wrote with an extraordinarily good knowledge of the facts and with a really penetrating sense of justice, but he lashed out as with a flail in regard to the injuries that had been inflicted. His tongue simply ran away with him—as, for example, when he heard and read about the erection of the well-known statue of Mayer at Heilbronn, and of the unveiling ceremony. " This puppet standing in the market square at Heilbronn is a final insult offered to the Galileo of the 19th century. The great man sits there with his legs crossed. But to portray him truly, in the frame of mind in which he would most probably be, he would have to be looking at the orator and at all the good friends below who erected this memorial, not sitting with his legs crossed but beating his breast in horror."

Having suffered much at the hands of newspapers, Dühring also became a violent anti-Semite. Here too he was ruthlessly consistent. For example, he wrote the pamphlet entitled *Die Ueberschätzung Lessings und dessen Anwaltschaft für die Juden,* in which murderous abuse is hurled at Lessing. It is this trait in Dühring that is responsible for his particular way of expounding literature.

If you want one day to give yourselves the treat of reading something about German literature that you will find nowhere else, that is totally different from other treatises on the subject, then take Dühring's two volumes entitled *Literaturgrössen* (Great Men of Letters). There you will find his strictly mathematical way of thinking and his astute perspicacity, applied to literature. In order, presumably, to make it plain how his way of thinking differs from that of others, he sees fit to rechristen the great figures of the German spiritual life. He speaks, in one chapter, of " Kothe " and " Schillerer," meaning Goethe and Schiller. Dühring writes " Kothe " and " Schillerer " and adheres to this throughout. The nomenclature he invents is often grotesque. " Intellectuaille " (connected with " canaille ") is how he always refers to people we call intellectualistic. The " Intellectuaille " —the Intellectuals. He uses similar expressions all the time. But let me assure you of this: a great deal in Dühring's writings is extraordinarily interesting.

I once had the following experience. When I was still on friendly terms with Frau Elizabeth Forster-Nietzsche and was working on unpublished writings of Nietzsche, there came into my hands the material dealing with the " Eternal Recurrence ", now long since printed.* Nietzsche's manuscripts are not very easy reading, but I came across a passage where I said to myself: This " Eternal Recurrence " has some definite source. And so I went over from the Archives, where Nietzsche's note-books were kept, to the Library, and looked up Dühring's *Wirklichkeitsphilosophie* (Philosophy of Reality), where, as I thought, I was quickly able to find this idea of " Eternal Recurrence ". I took the book from the shelves of the Library and found the passage—I knew it and found it at once—where Dühring argues that it is impossible for anyone with genuine knowledge of the material facts of the world to speak of a return of things, a return of constellations which once were there.

Dühring tried to disprove any such possibility. At the side of the passage in question was a word frequently written by Nietzsche in the margin of a book when he was using it to formulate a counter-idea. It was the word: " Ass "!

The familiar epithet was written in the margin of this particular page. In point of fact we can find in Dühring's writings a great deal that passed over, ingeniously, into Nietzsche's ideas. In saying this I hold nothing against Nietzsche. I am simply stating the facts as they are.

In respect of karma, the most striking thing about Dühring

* *Thus Spake Zarathustra*, Part III.

is that he was really able to think only mathematically. In philosophy, in political economy, in mathematics itself, he thinks mathematically, with mathematical precision and clarity. In natural science, too, he thinks with clarity but, again, in terms of mathematics. He is not a materialist, he is a mechanistic thinker. He conceives the world as mechanism. And moreover he had the courage to carry sincere convictions to their ultimate conclusions. For truth to tell, anyone who thinks as he did cannot write about Goethe and Schiller in any other way—leaving aside the abuse and taking only the essential substance of what is said.

So much for the fundamental trend of Dühring's thought. Add to this the blindness while he was still young, and the fact that he suffered no little personal injustice. He lost his post as lecturer at the University of Berlin. Well ... there were reasons! For example, in the second edition of his *History of Mechanics* he cast all restraint aside. The first edition had been quite tame in its treatment of the great figures in the field of mechanics, so tame that someone said he had written in a way which he thought would make it possible for a learned body to award him a prize. But in the second edition he no longer held himself in check; he let himself go and fairly filled in the gaps! Someone remarked— and Dühring often repeated it—that the Göttingen Academy had awarded a prize to the claws without recognising the lion behind the claws! But when the second edition appeared the lion had certainly come into the open!

In this second edition there were in truth some astounding passages, for example in connection with Julius Robert Mayer and his Galileo-destiny in the 19th century. On one occasion when Dühring was in a towering rage about this, he called a man he considered to be a plagiarist of Mayer—namely Hermann Helmholtz—so much " academic scaffolding," " wooden scaffolding." Later on he enlarged upon this theme. He edited a periodical *Der Personalist*, where every-thing had a strongly personal colouring. Here, for example, Dühring enlarges upon the reference to Helmholtz. He no longer speaks about wooden scaffolding, but when the

124

postmortem examination had revealed the presence of water in Helmholtz's brain, Dühring said that the empty-headedness had been quite obvious while the man was still alive and that there was no need to wait for confirmation until after his death! Refinement was certainly not one of Dühring's qualities. One cannot exactly say that he raged like a washer-woman. His way of abusing was not commonplace; neither was there real genius in it. It was something quite unique.

And now take all these factors together: the blindness, the mechanistic bent of mind, the persecution he certainly suffered—for the dismissal from the University was not altogether free from injustice, and indeed countless in-justices were done to him during his life. . . . All these things are connections of destiny which become really interesting only when we study them in the light of karma.

I have now given you a picture of these three personalities: Friedrich Theodor Vischer, the composer Schubert, and Eugen Dühring. Having outlined the biographical material to-day, I will speak to-morrow of the karmic connections.

VIII

I said yesterday that although it is a somewhat hazardous venture to speak of individual karmic connections, I intended to do so, and that I would take as examples the personalities of whom I gave you certain biographical details. Later on we shall also be able to study the karma of less representative personalities, but I have chosen, in the first place, examples which show clearly how in the karmic course of repeated phases of existence, the evolution of mankind as a whole goes forward. In modern civilisation we speak of history as if it were one continuous stream of happenings: events of the 20th century are related to events of the 19th century, these again to events of the 18th century, and so on. That it is men themselves who carry over things from one epoch of history to another, that the men now living have themselves carried over from earlier epochs what is to be found in the world and in life at the present time—this knowledge alone brings reality to light and reveals the true, inner connections in the historical life of mankind.

If we speak merely of " cause " and " effect," no real connection comes to light. The connecting threads running through the evolution of humanity are woven as human souls pass over from epochs in the remote past to more recent times, entering again and again into new incarnations on the earth.

These connecting threads can be perceived in all their significance when we study really representative personalities.

In the lecture yesterday I spoke, firstly, of the aestheticist Friedrich Theodor Vischer, the " Swabian Vischer " as he is called, telling you something of his character. I said that I shall choose only examples that I have actually investigated. These investigations are a matter of vision, and are pursued by means of the spiritual faculties of which I have spoken so

127

often and about which you can read in anthroposophical literature. Accordingly the only possible way of describing these things is that of narrative, for in this domain it is only what presents itself to direct vision that can be communicated. The moment we turn from one earthly life to an earlier life in the past, all intellectual reasoning comes to a standstill. Vision alone is the criterion here. A last vestige of intellectual understanding is possible when it is a matter of relating earthly life to the last phase of existence between death and rebirth from which it has directly proceeded—that is, to the life of soul-and-spirit just before the descent to earth. Here, up to a point, an intellectual approach is possible. When, however, it is a matter of showing the relation between one earthly life and a preceding incarnation, this can be done only in the form of narrative, for vision is the sole criterion. And if in contemplating a personality like Friedrich Theodor Vischer one is able to apprehend what is eternal in him— what passes over from one earthly life to another—then such a personality as he was in an earlier incarnation will emerge into one's field of vision, provided always that the right currents can be found in the whole series of earthly lives. Investigation leads back, first of all, of course, to the pre-earthly experiences. But in speaking now I shall give second place to these pre-earthly experiences and indicate how, behind the earthly lives of the three personalities in question, their previous incarnations can be perceived.

In undertaking such investigations it is absolutely essential to get rid of all preconceived notions. If, because of some opinion or view we may hold concerning the present or the last earthly life of a human being, we imagine that it is justifiable to argue intellectually that because of what he is now, he must have been this or that in an earlier incarnation —if we make judgments of this kind, we shall go astray, or at any rate it will be very easy to go astray. To base an intellectual judgment of one incarnation upon another in this way would be just as if we were to go into a house for the first time, look out of the windows facing north, and seeing trees outside were to conclude from these trees what the trees look like from the windows facing south. What must be done is to go to the south windows, see the trees there and look at them with entirely unbiased eyes.

In the same way, all intellectual reasoning must cease when it is a matter of apprehending the Imaginations which correspond to the earlier earthly lives of the personalities in question.

In the case of Friedrich Theodor Vischer, one is led back to the last incarnation of importance—in the intervening time there may have been one or another unimportant or possibly brief earthly life, but for the moment that is of no consequence—one is led back to the incarnation in which the karma of his present life was prepared—I mean " present " in the wider sense, for as you know, Vischer died at the end of the eighties of the 19th century. The incarnation in which the karma of his latest earthly life was prepared lies somewhere about the 8th century A.D. We see him among the Moorish-Arabian peoples who crossed over at this time from Africa to Sicily and there came into conflict with the peoples who were making their way down to Sicily from the north.

The essential point is that in this previous incarnation of importance, the individuality of whom I am speaking had received a thoroughly Arabian education, Arabian in every detail, containing all the artistic, perhaps also the inartistic elements in Arabism; it was characterised, too, by the vital energy with which in those days Arabism forced its way to Europe; and, above all, it brought this individuality into close human relationship with a large number of other men belonging to the same race.

This individuality, who afterwards lived in the 19th century as Friedrich Theodor Vischer, tried in the 8th century to establish close comradeship with many men belonging to the same Arabian stock and the same Arabian culture, who had already made strong contacts with Europe, were endeavouring to establish themselves in Sicily, and had to face heavy fighting; or rather it was really more the Europeans who had to face the fighting. The individuality we are considering

129

took a full share in these conflicts. One may say that he was a person of genius—in the sense in which genius was conceived in those times. This individuality then, is to be found in the 8th century A.D.

Then he passes through the gate of death into the life between death and rebirth, during which there is naturally intimate fellowship with the souls with whom one has been together on earth. Here, in the spiritual world, were the souls with whom this individuality had tried, as I have just told you, to establish close relationship.

Now between these human beings—in language that has been coined for earthly relationships it is difficult to find expressions for describing supersensible conditions—between the human souls with whom this individuality was now together, after he and they had passed through the gate of death, there existed through all the following centuries, right into the 19th century, a spirit-bond, a spiritual tie.

You will have understood from the lecture I gave here a week ago that what takes place on earth is lived through in advance by the Beings of the highest Hierarchies, by the Seraphim, Cherubim and Thrones, and that a human being who is passing through the life between death and a new birth looks *down* to a heaven of soul and spirit as we look *up* to the heavens. There, in that heaven of soul and spirit, the Seraphim, Cherubim and Thrones live through what subsequently becomes our destiny, what is brought to realisation as our destiny when we descend again to the earth.

Now, in the conditions obtaining in the spiritual world, it was foreseen by the souls belonging to the community into which the individuality we are studying had been drawn, that through the coming centuries it would be their destiny to preserve a line of progress that would be quite uninfluenced by Christianity. What I am now saying will seem very strange, for the idea often prevails that the ordering of the world is as simple as we humans like to have it in everything we arrange ourselves. But the ordering of the world is by no means so simple. While on the one hand the mightiest of all impulses poured from the Mystery of Golgotha into the whole

130

of Earth evolution, on the other hand it was necessary that what had been contained in earthly evolution *before* the Mystery of Golgotha should not be allowed at once to perish; it was necessary that what was, I will not say " anti-Christian " but " non-Christian," should be allowed to stream on through the centuries.

And the task of sustaining this stream of culture for Europe —as it were of enabling a phase of culture not yet Christian to continue on into the Christian centuries—fell to a number of individuals who were born into Arabism in the 7th and 8th centuries A.D. Arabism was not, of course, directly Christian, but neither had it remained as backward as the old heathen religions. In a certain direction it had made steady progress through the centuries. A number of souls born into this stream were to carry forward in the spiritual world, untouched by the conditions prevailing on earth, that which the spirit of man, separated from Christianity, can know, feel and experience. They were to encounter Christianity only later, in later epochs of earthly evolution. And it is in truth an experience of shattering grandeur, full of deep significance, to see how a large community lived on in the spiritual world removed from the development of Christianity, until in the 19th century the majority of these souls came down to incarnation on earth. As you may suppose, they were very different individualities, with every variety of talent and disposition.

Friedrich Theodor Vischer was one of the first souls from this community to descend in the 19th century.* And he was as remote as can be from any possibility of direct experience of Christianity.

On the other hand, while still in his pre-earthly existence, he was able to receive impulses from those leading spirits who had been more or less near to Christianity but whose views of the world and conceptual life had developed in a direction *not* primarily and intrinsically Christian.

For a soul such as the one we now have in mind, the incarnation in the 7th/8th century was an especially good

---

* Vischer was born in 1807 and died in 1887.

131

preparation—(it is of course paradoxical to speak of these things as one speaks of earthly affairs, but as I said, I intend to make the venture)—for coming together in the spiritual world with souls like that of Spinoza and others of a similar type, and with a large number of bearers of non-Christian culture, particularly, too, of Cabbalistic culture, who died during those centuries and came up into the spiritual world.

Thus prepared, this particular soul came into earthly existence in the 19th century, rather earlier than the others. All the others, for the reason that they descended somewhat later, became bearers of the natural-scientific outlook prevailing in the second half of the 19th century. For in point of fact the secret of the peculiar evolution of natural-scientific thinking in the second half of the 19th century is that wellnigh all the bearers of this stream at that time had been Arabians in their previous incarnations of importance; they were companions of the individuality who then came down as Friedrich Theodor Vischer. But Vischer came down earlier than they—it was like a premature birth in the sense of soul-and-spirit.

This, moreover, was grounded deeply in his karma, owing to his association, before his descent to earthly life, with the souls with whom Hegel was connected. With these souls, too, Friedrich Theodor Vischer had been associated in the spiritual world. This expressed itself in a strong personal bent for what Hegelianism became on earth, and protected him from growing into a purely materialistic-mechanistic conception of the world. If he had been born somewhat later, as were his companions in the spiritual life, he too, as an aestheticist, would in the natural course of things have headed straight for materialism. He was protected from this by his experiences in pre-earthly life and by his earlier descent to earth. But he could not adhere permanently to this Hegelian influence. And that is why he came to write the destructive critique of his own aesthetics—because here was something that was not quite in the line of his karma but was the result of a deflection of his karma. It would have been entirely in line with his karma to have been born at the same

132

time as men who were steeped in the natural-scientific thinking of the second half of the 19th century, men who had been his associates in the earlier incarnation, belonging, as he did, to Arabism. His karma would have led him naturally to the same orientation of thinking.

The strange fact is that through a deflection of karma—which will be adjusted in later earthly lives—Friedrich Theodor Vischer was torn away from the straightforward line of his karma. This deflection was determined by his pre-earthly existence, not by his earthly karma. But when he reached a certain age he could no longer sustain it; he was impelled to enter right into his karma. And so he rejects his five-volume work on aesthetics and succumbs to the temptation of approaching the subject in the way of which the natural scientists would approve. In his first work on aesthetics he looks down from above, starting from principles and then passing to sense-phenomena. This he now criticises root and branch. He wants now to build from below upwards, starting from material facts and gradually rising to principles. And we witness a tremendous struggle: Vischer working at the destruction of his own aesthetics! We see how karma had been deflected and how he is hurled back into it, led to those whose companion he had been in a previous earthly life.

It is shattering in its significance to see how Vischer never really makes progress with this second work on aesthetics, how a kind of chaos seems to creep into the whole of his spiritual life. I told you yesterday about his curiously philistine attitude even towards Goethe's *Faust*. It is all due to the fact that he feels unsure of himself and is striving to get back to his old companions. But we must remember how strongly the unconscious works in karma. At a higher stage, of course, it becomes conscious. We must also remember how deeply certain philistine scientists hated Goethe's *Faust*! I told you yesterday what Du Bois-Reymond said on the subject: that it would have been much more sensible of Goethe to let Faust make some real discovery rather than call up spirits, evoke the Earth-Spirit, associate with Mephistopheles or seduce young girls and not marry them afterwards. Du Bois-Reymond regards all this as tomfoolery. According to him, Goethe should have presented a hero who invents an electrical machine or an air pump! Then there would have been social propriety about it all and the hero would have become Mayor of Magdeburg. Above all, there ought to have been no Gretchen-tragedy, and instead of the Prison Scene a correct and proper civic wedding! Well . . . it is a point of view that is not without justification; but it was certainly not what Goethe had in mind!

Friedrich Theodor Vischer, as I said, was not completely sure of himself after his karma had been deflected in this way. But something was always pulling him back, and unconsciously, although he was a really free spirit, he was always delighted when he heard the philistines running down Goethe's *Faust*. He was witty, of course, and clever, and it was like snowballing going on between them. It is precisely when one observes things about a human being that are more a matter of vision, that one lights upon the Imaginations which lead behind the scenes of material existence.

Truly it is a grand spectacle! There, on the one side, stand the philistines of the first order, like Du Bois-Reymond and the others, saying that Goethe ought to have represented Faust as Mayor of Magdeburg, inventing the electrical machine and the air-pump, and marrying Gretchen—verily these are philistines of the first order! Something is at work in the subconscious, because a karmic connection is in operation here. All these men had been Moors, associated with Vischer in Arabism. He was attracted by it all, he felt related to it . . . and yet in another respect he was not. In the intervening time he had come into contact with other streams which had brought about a deflection of his karma. And now when the philistines of the first order threw their snowballs, he threw back his, saying that someone ought to write a thesis on a subject like the relation of Frau Christine von Goethe's chilblains to the symbolic-allegorical figures in the second part of *Faust*! That, you will agree, is philistinism with a touch of real wit in it, it is philistinism of the second order!

To assess these things at their true value is a matter of vision, not of merely intellectual apprehension.

In what I have told you of Vischer, my aim, to begin with, was to give you some indication—I shall return to these things again—of how the one earthly life can be understood from foregoing earthly lives.

There was something extraordinarily significant about the figure of Vischer going about in Stuttgart. I mentioned to you yesterday the wonderful blue eyes, the reddish-brown beard, the arms held out in the way I described. The Imagination of him, however, did not tally with the physical stature of the Swabian Vischer as he went about Stuttgart, for even to occult sight he did not look like a reincarnated Arabian. Again and again I left the matter alone, because one becomes —I cannot say " sceptical " in regard to one's visions, but one does become distrustful, one wants to have definite confirmation. Again and again I let the matter drop, until the riddle was solved in the following way.

In the 7th/8th century—that was also a male incarnation— this individuality regarded the men from the North, especially those he encountered in Sicily, as his ideal. In those days, as you may imagine, it was very easy to be carried away by people one greatly admired. And so he " caught " as it were, his bodily characteristics in the later incarnation from those against whom he had once waged war. Here is the solution of the riddle in regard to his physical stature.

In the last lecture we considered a second personality, namely, *Franz Schubert*, in connection with his friend Spaun, and with his own volcanic nature which on rare occasions, such as the one I related to you, could flare up in rage, making him into a thorough brawler; on the other hand he was extraordinarily tender and sensitive; he was like a sleep-walker, writing down his lovely melodies directly after waking in the morning. It was extremely difficult to get a picture of this personality, but the connection with Spaun gave the clue. For in the case of Schubert himself, when one looks back in the occult field and tries to find something definite, one has the feeling that he gives one the slip—if I may use this

colloquialism. It is not easy to go back to his former incarna-
.tion; he eludes one all the time.

There is in truth something of a contrast here with the
destiny of Schubert's works after his death. At the time of
Schubert's death his compositions were very little known;
only a few people had heard of him. After the lapse of some
years, however, he became more and more renowned, until
in the seventies and eighties of last century, fresh works of his
were published every year. It was very interesting: suddenly,
long after his death, Schubert turned out to be a most prolific
composer. New works of his were constantly appearing.

When, however, we look back spiritually from Schubert's
life in the 19th century into his earlier earthly life, the tracks
disappear; it is not easy to find him.

On the other hand it is comparatively easy to find the
tracks in the case of Baron von Spaun. And this line also
led back to the 8th or 9th century A.D., to Spain. He was a
Prince of Castile who had a name for being extraordinarily
wise. He busied himself with astrology and with astronomy
in the form current in those days, amending and drawing up
astronomical tables. At a certain time in his life this Prince
was .forced to flee from his home, and he found refuge
among those who were actually the bitterest enemies of the
Castilian population at that time, namely the Moors.

He was obliged to stay here for a considerable time, and he
formed a relationship of great tenderness and intimacy with
a Moorish personality in whom the individuality of the later
Franz Schubert was then incarnated. And this Prince of
Castile would certainly have met with his end had it not been
for the tender-spirited personality among the Moors who
cared for him with every kindness. His earthly life was thus
safeguarded for many years, to the great joy of them both.

What I am now relating to you is utterly remote from
intellectual deduction in any shape or form. I have indicated
the roundabout way which the research had to take. But
along this roundabout way one is led to the fact that in
Franz Schubert we have a reincarnated Moorish personality,
one who had little opportunity of cultivating musical talent

in his life among the Moors, but who, on the other hand, steeped himself with impassioned longing in whatever was to be found in the way of art and, I will not say of subtle "thinking" but rather of subtle "reasoning," which in the train of Arabic culture had come from Asia, passed across Africa and finally reached Spain.

During that incarnation this personality developed the gentle, unassuming and yet vital flexibility of soul which quickened to life the poetic, dreamlike phantasy in the later incarnation as Franz Schubert. On the other hand this personality was obliged to take part in the fierce conflicts now again taking place between the Moors and the non-Moorish inhabitants of Castile, Aragon, and so forth. And this accounted for the suppressed emotion which like a pent-up stream burst forth—but only in unusual circumstances—during the Schubert-existence.

It seems to me that just as the earlier life of Friedrich Theodor Vischer can be understood only when one can view it against the background of Arabism, so the essence of Schubert's music, especially the undertone of many of his songs, can be discerned only when one perceives (I have not constructed anything, it arises from the facts themselves) that there is something spiritual in this music, something Asiatic which was shone upon for a time by the desert sun, took on greater definition in Europe, was carried through the spiritual world between death and rebirth and as something essentially human, removed from all the artificialities of society, came to birth again in a penniless schoolteacher.

The third personality of whom I spoke yesterday was Eugen Dühring.* I shall give brief indications only, for we can always return to these subjects again. Eugen Dühring was of particular interest to me because as a young man I was deeply engrossed in the study of his writings. I was fascinated by his works on physics and mathematics, especially by the treatise *Neue Grundmittel und Erfindungen zur Analysis, Algebra, Funktionsrechnung*, and by his treatment of the law of corresponding boiling points. I was irritated to distraction by a book such as *Sache, Leben und*

* Born 1833, died 1901.   137

Feinde which is a sort of autobiography. There is something terribly self-complacent about it, self-complacent to the point of genius; not to mention traits which came out in utterly malicious pamphlets such as *Die Ueberschätzung Lessings und dessen Anwaltschaft für die Juden.* On the other hand I could admire Dühring's *History of Mechanics* as long as the lion was not in evidence, but only the lion's claws. There was, however, one unpleasant impression: for a history of mechanics, too much is said about all the gossip associated with Frau Helmholtz; abuse is hurled at Hermann Helmholtz, but the emphasis is upon the gossip that went on in the circle around Frau Helmholtz. Well . . . such things do happen; gossip goes on in all kinds of circles! . . . As I have said, I experienced every shade of feeling in regard to Dühring and his writings: respect, deep appreciation, criticism, irritation. And you will understand the desire to see how these traits had developed against the background of at any rate the immediately preceding earthly life.

But here again it was not easy, and at first—I have no wish to keep back these things—at first, the pictures were deceptive. Deceptive pictures arise very easily, because everything often depends upon starting from what is actually the most significant feature in some particular life of a human being in order to be led back along the right path. And in the case of Dühring it was a long time before I succeeded in finding any really significant feature.

The procedure I adopted was as follows.—I pictured to myself everything about him that appealed to me most, namely his materialistic-mechanistic conception of the world—materialistic, but yet, in a certain respect, spiritual, intellectually spiritual. I turned over in my mind how it all has to do with a finite world of space, a finite world of time; I constructed Dühring's whole conception of the world again for myself. That is not difficult. But when one has done it and looks back to earlier incarnations, numbers and numbers come into view and again there is delusion. One finds nothing essential; countless incarnations appear, but there cannot, of course, possibly have been so many: they are

138

nothing but reflections of the present incarnation. It is just as if you were to have mirrors in a room, one here and another there: you would see numberless reflections. Then I went on to ponder with all intensity: What *is* Dühring's world-conception in reality, expressed in terms of clear thought? For the time being I left aside all the spiteful criticism, the abuse and other such non-essentials. I left all that aside and concentrated upon what is really grand and impressive in a world-conception which, as such, has always been antipathetic to me, but which, on account of the way in which Dühring presented it, attracted me. I pictured all this vividly to myself and then tried to get a clear grasp of the reality. From a certain age onwards he was totally blind. A blind man does not see the world, and his mental image of it is quite different from that of a man with sight. In point of fact, ordinary materialists, ordinary mechanistic thinkers, are on a different level altogether from Dühring. In comparison with them, Dühring has genius. All these men who have evolved conceptions of the world, Vogt, Büchner, Moleschott, Spiller, Wiessner and the rest—" twelve to the dozen " as the saying goes—with them it is a very different matter. The way in which Dühring builds up his world-conception is utterly different. We can perceive, too, that the urge to give a certain shape to this view of the world was in him even before he became blind, and it really tallied with the fundamental trend of his mind only when he had lost his sight and space was dark around him. For the principles according to which Dühring builds up his world-conception belong essentially to dark space. It is a fallacy to imagine that this was the work of a man with sight.

But just think of it. In Dühring this is intrinsic *truth*. Other men—twelve dozen of them if you like—have evolved such conceptions of the world, but with Dühring there is a difference: with Dühring it is true. The others have sight and construct pictures of the world as if they were blind; Dühring *is* blind and evolves his world-conception as one who is blind. And that is an astonishing thing! If one realises what it means, if one observes this man and knows:

here is someone who in his soul-evolution was like a blind man, whose outlook becomes mechanistic because of his blindness—then one finds him again. Two incarnations come into consideration here. We find him associated with the movement in the Eastern Church, about the 8th or 9th century A.D., which at one period was iconoclastic, bent upon the destruction of all images, and then, later on, reinstated them. In Constantinople, particularly, this conflict developed between religion employing pictures and images, and religion in which none were permitted. And there we find the individuality who was born in a later age as Eugen Dühring, battling ardently, good fighter as he was, for a cultural life devoid of pictures and images. Here, manifesting in purely physical conflict, one can see all that later comes to expression in words.

One point was extraordinarily interesting to me. A strange word occurs in the second volume of the work on Julius Robert Mayer. One actually *sees* the whole thing! In the earlier incarnation, when Dühring was engaged in destroying images, he had a special way of brandishing his scimitar, the hooked scimitar which already then was being tried out and developed. In the book on Mayer—these things, you know, often turn on pictorial details—I found a word that seemed to ring in unison with the scimitar. There is a chapter in this book entitled *Schlichologisches* (" trick-ology "). " Trick-ology " in German University life and so forth—getting in from the side by a cunning manoeuvre.

Dühring coins the word " *Schlichologisches*," as well as the amusing expression " *Intellectuaille*," connected with *canaille*. He invents all kinds of words. As I said, details that seem quite unimportant may be very revealing. And paradoxical as it may appear, one does not really arrive at the connecting links between different earthly lives unless one has an eye and a feeling for symptoms of this kind. Anyone who cannot discern a man's character from the way he walks, how he steps on the soles of his feet, will not easily make progress in such matters as those dealt with in the present lectures. One must be able to see the very swing of the scimitar transferred into words that were coined by this individuality in his subsequent life.

Dühring was always heaping abuse on the savants—" men of unlearning," as he calls them. He said he would be thankful if there were no more names to remind him of ancient erudition. He wants no logic, he wants anti-logic; no Sophia, but anti-Sophia; no science, but anti-science. He says explicitly that he would like best of all to make everything " anti." Now in the incarnation before the one when he was a rabid iconoclast, this man who so fiercely abused everything in the way of erudition had belonged to the School of the Greek Stoics, was himself a Stoic philosopher. In days of antiquity Dühring was himself one of the kind of men he now abused so vehemently; in the third incarnation back he was a professed philosopher, a Stoic philosopher at that, therefore one who in a certain sense withdrew from earthly life.

What dawned upon me first of all was that very many of Dühring's thoughts, or rather the forms in which his thoughts are expressed, are to be found in the Stoics! The matter is not, of course, as simple as all that. Indeed a whole course of lectures might be given on the forms of thought in Dühring and in the Stoics.

Thus we are led back, first, to the age of iconoclasm in the east of Europe about the 9th century A.D., when Dühring was a rabid iconoclast; then to the 3rd century B.C., the period of Stoic philosophy in ancient Greece.

And now again it is astounding: this Stoic, who makes no demands upon life, who holds back from everything that is not absolutely essential to life, renounces earthly sight in the second of the subsequent incarnations. And in this he brings truth to expression, for he illustrates in a magnificent way the blindness of the modern conception of the world.

Whatever may be one's attitude to Dühring's conception of the world, the moving tragedy of it is that Dühring personifies what the world-conception prevailing in the 19th century truly is; he expresses it through his very make-up as a man. The Stoic, who would not face the world as it is, becomes blind; the iconoclast, the destroyer of images, who will not tolerate imagery, makes the history of literature and poetry into what it became in Dühring's two volumes on *Great Men of Letters*, where not only are Goethe and Schiller put aside but where at most a man like Bürger plays any definite rôle. Here we have the truth of what is presented elsewhere in a false light. For men assert that the mechanistic thought, the materialism of the second half of the 19th century, *sees*. There lies the untruth, for materialism does not see; materialism is blind. And Dühring presents it as it truly is.

And so a representative personality, viewed in the right light, is an illustration of world-historic karma, the karma of civilisation as represented by its conception of the world in the second half of the 19th century.

In the next lecture we will speak further of these matters.

IX

In these lectures we are speaking of karma, of the paths of human destiny, and in the last lecture we studied certain connections which can throw light on the way in which destiny works through the course of successive earthly lives. I have decided—although needless to say it was a decision fraught with risk—to speak in detail of such karmic connections, and to-day we will carry our studies a little further.

You will have seen that in describing karmic connections it is necessary to mention many details in the life and character of a human being which in the ordinary way might escape attention. In the case of Dühring, I pointed out how a bodily peculiarity of one incarnation became a particular trend and attitude of soul in the next. For it is a fact that when one presses through to the spiritual worlds in search of the true being of man, the spiritual loses its abstractness and becomes full of force; on the other hand, the corporeality, all that comes to expression in the bodily nature of man, loses, one may truthfully say, its materiality; it assumes a spiritual significance and acquires a definite place in the interconnections of human life.

How does destiny actually work ? Destiny arises from the *whole* being of man. What a man seeks in life as the result of a karmic urge, and which then comes to him in the form of destiny, depends upon the fact that forces of destiny, as they pass from life to life, influence and condition the very composition of the blood in its more delicate qualities and regulate the activity of the nerves; to their working is due also the instinctive sensitiveness of the soul to this or that influence. We shall not easily find our way into the innermost nature of karmic connections if we do not pay attention—with the eye of the soul, of course—to the particular mannerisms of an individual. Believe me, for the study of karma it is just as important to be interested in a gesture of the hand as in some great spiritual talent. It is just as important to be able to observe—from the spiritual side (astral body and ego) —how a man sits down on a chair as to observe, let us say, how he discharges his moral obligations. If a man is given to frowning, to knitting his brow, this may be just as important as whether he is virtuous or the reverse.

Much that in ordinary life seems to be quite insignificant is of very great importance when we begin to consider destiny and observe how it weaves its web from life to life; while many a thing in this or the other human being that appears to us particularly important becomes of negligible significance.

Generally speaking, it is not, as you know, very easy to pay real attention to bodily pecularities. They are there and we must learn to observe them naturally without wounding our fellow-men—as we certainly shall do if we observe merely for observation's sake. That must never be. Everything must arise entirely of itself. When, however, we have trained our powers of attention and perception, individual peculiarities do show themselves in every human being, peculiarities which may be accounted trifling but are of paramount importance in connection with the study of karma. A really penetrating observation of human beings in respect of their karmic connections is possible only when we can discern these significant peculiarities.

Some decades ago, a personality whose inner, spiritual life as well as his outer life were intensely interesting to me, was the philosopher *Eduard von Hartmann.*

When I try to study von Hartmann's life in such a way as to lead to a perception of his karma, I have to picture to myself what was of value in his life somewhat in the following way.—Eduard von Hartmann, the philosopher of the Unconscious, was really an explosive influence in philosophy, but thinkers of the 19th century—pardon me if I sound critical, I mean it not unkindly—received the effects of this explosive effect in the realm of the spirit with extraordinary apathy. Indeed, the men of the 19th century simply cannot be wakened—and I include, of course, the 20th century that has now begun; it is impossible to shake them out of their phlegmatic attitude towards anything that really stirs the world inwardly. No enthusiasm of any depth is to be found in this phlegmatic age—phlegmatic, that is to say, in respect of spiritual life.

In another recent series of lectures I gave a picture of the encounter between the Roman world and the world of the Northern Germanic peoples at the time of the migrations, at the time when Christianity was beginning to spread to the North from the southerly regions of Greece and Rome. You have only to picture these physical forefathers of Middle and Southern Europe truly, and you will get some impression of the inner, dynamic vigour which once spurred men to action in the world. The Germanic tribes whom the Romans encountered in the early Christian centuries knew what it was to live in union with the spiritual powers of nature. The attitude of these men to the Spiritual was quite different from ours; in most of them, of course, there was still an instinctive inclination towards the Spiritual. And whereas we to-day speak for the most part phlegmatically, so that one word simply follows another, as though speech contained nothing *real*, these people poured out what they actually experienced into words and speech. For them the surging roar of the wind was as much a physical gesture, a manifestation of soul-and-spirit, as when a man moves his arm. In the surge of the wind and in the flickering of the light in the wind, they saw an expression of Wodan. And when they carried these realities over into speech, when they clothed them in language, they imbued their words with the *character* of what they experienced. If we were to express it in modern words, saying " *Wodan weht im Winde* " (Wodan weaves in the wind)— and the words were almost similar in olden times—there the weaving activity pours into the language itself. Think of how this direct participation in the life and forces of nature vibrates and pulsates in the words, how it surges into them! When a man of those times looked up to the heavens and heard the thunder roaring and rumbling out of the clouds, and behind this nature-gesture of the thunder beheld the

145

corresponding spiritual reality of being, he brought the whole experience to expression in the words " *Donner* (or *Donar*) *dröhnt im Donner* " (Thor rumbles in the thunder)—for thus we may hear, transposed into modern language, words that still echo the sound of the ancient speech. And just as these men felt the Spiritual in the workings of nature and expressed it in their speech, so did they also express their experience of the God who aided them when they went forth to battle, who lived in their very limbs and in their whole bearing and action. They held their mighty shields before them, shouting the words like a war-cry. And the fact that spirits, whether good spirits or demons, stormed into the words which rose and fell with powerful resonance—all this they expressed as they rushed forward to attack, in the words: " *Ziu Zwingt Zwist.*" Spoken behind the shield, spoken with all the rage and lust of battle, that really was like the breaking of a storm! You must imagine it shouted as it were against the shields by thousands of voices at once. In those early centuries, when the peoples of the South came into conflict with those pouring down from Middle Europe, it was not the outer course of the battle that had the decisive effect. No—it was rather this mighty shout accompanying the attack against the Romans! For in those early times it was this shout that filled the people coming from the South with a terrible fear. Knees trembled before the " *Ziu Zwingt Zwist*," bellowed forth by a thousand throats behind the shields.

And so we are bound to say: these same men are there again in the world to-day, but they have become phlegmatic! Many a man alive to-day bellowed and roared in those days of yore but has now become utterly phlegmatic, has adopted the attitude of soul typical of the 19th and 20th centuries. But if those men were to return in the mood of soul that inspired them in the days when they yelled their war-cry, they would feel like donning a nightcap in their present incarnation, for they would say: This phlegmatic apathy out of which people simply cannot be roused, belongs properly under a nightcap; bed is the place for it, not the arena of human action!

I say this only because I want to indicate how little inclination there was among the men of von Hartmann's time to let themselves be roused by an explosive force like that contained in his *Philosophy of the Unconscious*. He spoke, to begin with, of how all that is conscious in man, all his conscious thinking is of less significance than that which works and weaves unconsciously in him, as it does in nature, and can never be raised into consciousness. Of clairvoyant Imagination and Intuition, Eduard von Hartmann knew nothing; he did not know that the unconscious can penetrate into the sphere of human cognition. And so he asserts that what is really essential in the world and in life remains in the unconscious. This very reasoning, however, gives him the ground for his view that the world in which we live is the worst world imaginable. He carried his pessimism even further than Schopenhauer and reached the conclusion that the evolution of culture must culminate in the destruction of the whole of earth-evolution. He would not insist, he said, that this would happen in the immediate future, because that would not give time to apply all that will be necessary for carrying the destruction so far that no human civilisation—which in any case, according to his view, is worthless—will be left. And he dreamed—you will find it in his *Philosophy of the Unconscious*—he dreamed of how men will ultimately invent a huge machine which they will be able to lower deeply enough into the earth to produce a terrific explosion, scattering the whole earth in fragments through universal space.

It is true that many people have been enthusiastic about this *Philosophy of the Unconscious*. But when they come to talk about it, one does not feel that it has taken any real hold of them. A statement like Hartmann's can, of course, be made, and there is something powerful in the mere fact of its utterance—but people quote it as though they were making a casual remark, and that is the really terrible thing.

Yes, there was actually a philosopher who spoke in this way. And this same philosopher went on to expound the subject of human morality on earth. It was his work *Phänomenologie des sittlichen Bewusstseins* (Phenomenology

147

of the Moral Consciousness) that interested me most of all. He also wrote a book entitled *Das religiöse Bewusstsein der Menschheit* (The Religious Consciousness of Mankind), and another on Aesthetics—in fact he wrote a very great deal.* And it was all extraordinarily interesting, particularly where one could not agree with him.

In the case of such a man one may very naturally desire to know the connections of his destiny. One may try, perhaps, to make a deep study of his philosophy, to glean from his philosophical thoughts some idea of his earlier earthly lives, but all such attempts will be fruitless. Nevertheless a personality like Eduard von Hartmann interested me in the highest degree.

When one has occultism in one's very bones—if I may put it so—the impulses for looking at things in the right way arise of themselves. And here one is confronted with the following circumstances.—Eduard von Hartmann was a soldier, an officer. The *Kürschner Directory*, besides recording his Doctorate of Philosophy and other academic degrees, put him down until the day of his death as " First Lieutenant." Eduard von Hartmann was an officer in the Prussian Army and is said to have been a very good one.

From a certain day onwards this fact seemed to me more significant in connection with the threads of his destiny than all the details of his philosophy. As for his philosophy—well, one is inclined to accept certain things and reject others. But there is nothing much in that; everyone who knows a little philosophy can do the same and the result will not amount to anything very striking. But now let us ask ourselves: How comes it that a Prussian officer, who was a good officer, who took very little interest in philosophy while he was in the Army but was much more concerned with sword-exercises—how comes it that such a man turns into a representative philosopher of his age ?

It was due to the fact that an illness left him with an affliction of the knee from which he suffered for the rest of his life, and he was invalided out of the Army on a pension. At

* With the exception of the *Philosophy of the Unconscious* the works of Eduard von Hartmann mentioned in this lecture have not been translated into English.

148

times he was quite unable to walk and was obliged to recline with his legs stretched out on a sofa. And then, after having imbibed contemporary scholarship, he wrote one philosophical work after another. Eduard von Hartmann's philosophical writings are a whole library in themselves; his output was prodigious.

Now when I came to study this personality, it dawned upon me one day that there was very special importance in the onset of this knee affliction. The fact that at a certain age the man began to suffer from an affliction of the knee interested me much more than his transcendental realism, or even than his famous saying: "First there was the religion of the Father, then the religion of the Son, and in the future there will come the religion of the Spirit." Such sayings show ability and astuteness of mind, but they were to be met with at every street corner, so to say, in the 19th century. But for a man to become a philosopher through contracting, while he was a Lieutenant, an infirmity of the knee—that is a most significant fact. Moreover until we can go back to such things and not allow ourselves to be dazzled by what appears to be the most striking feature in a man's life, we shall not be able to discover the karmic connections.

When I was able to bring the affliction of the knee into its right relation with the whole personality, I began to perceive how destiny manifested in the life of this man. And then I could go back. It was not by starting from the head of Eduard von Hartmann, but from the knee, that I found the way to his earlier incarnations. What seems to be of most importance in the life between birth and death does *not*, as a rule, afford the most reliable starting-point.

And now, what is the connection? Man as he stands before us as a physical being in earthly life, is a threefold being. He has his nerves-and-senses organism, which is concentrated mainly in the head but at the same time extends over the whole body. He has his rhythmic organisation, which manifests particularly clearly in the rhythm of the breath and of the circulation of the blood, but again extends over the whole human being and comes to expression everywhere within him. And thirdly, he has his motor organisation which is connected with the limbs, with the functioning of metabolism, with the reconstruction of the substances of the body and so forth. Man is a threefold being.

And then in regard to the whole constitution of life, we come to realise that on the journey through births and deaths, what we are accustomed to consider in earthly life as the most important part of man, namely the head, becomes of comparatively little importance shortly after death. The head that in the physical world is the most essentially human part of man, really expends itself in physical existence; whereas the rest of the organism—which, physically speaking, is subordinate—is of higher importance in the spiritual world. In his head, man is most of all physical and least of all spiritual. In the other members of his organism, in the rhythmic organisation and in the limbs-organisation, he is more spiritual. He is most spiritual of all in his motor organisation, in the activity of his limbs.

Now gifts and talents belonging to the head are lost comparatively soon after death. On the other hand, the soul-and-spirit which, in the realm of the unconscious, belongs to the lower part of the human organism, assumes great importance between death and a new birth. But whereas, speaking generally, the organism of man apart from the head becomes, in respect of its spiritual form, its spiritual content, the head of the next incarnation, it is also true that what is of the nature of *will* in the head, works especially into the limbs in the next incarnation. A man who is lazy in his thinking in one incarnation will most certainly be no fast runner in the next: the laziness of thinking becomes slowness of limb; and, *vice versa*, slowness of limb in the present incarnation comes to expression in sluggish, lazy thinking in the next.

Thus a metamorphosis, an interchange, takes place between the three members of the human being in passing over from one incarnation to another.

What I am telling you here is not put forward as a theory; it is based on the very facts of life. And in the case of Eduard von Hartmann, as soon as I turned my attention to the

150

affliction of the knee, I was guided to his earlier incarnation, during which at a certain moment in his life he had a kind of sunstroke. In respect of destiny, this sunstroke was the cause that led in the next earthly life, through metamorphosis, to an infirmity of the knee—the sunstroke being, as you will realise, an affliction of the *head*. One day he was no longer able to think. He had a kind of paralysis of the brain, and this came to expression in the next incarnation as an affliction of one of the limbs. Now the destiny that led to paralysis of the brain was due to the following circumstances.—This individuality was one of those who went to the East with the Crusades and fought over in Asia against the Turks and Asiatic peoples, acquiring, however, a tremendous admiration for the latter. The Crusaders encountered very much that was great and sublime in the East, and the individuality of whom we are speaking absorbed it all with deep admiration. And now he came across a man concerning whom he felt instinctively that he had had something to do with him in a still earlier life. The account, so to speak, that had now to be settled between this and the still earlier incarnation, was a moral account. The metamorphosis of the sunstroke in one incarnation into the affliction of the knee in the next appears at first to be a purely physical matter, but when it is a question of destiny we are invariably led back to something that appertains to the moral life. This individuality bore with him from a still earlier incarnation the impulse to wage a fierce battle with the man whom he now encountered, and in the heat of the blazing sun he set about persecuting his opponent. The persecution was unjust, and it recoiled upon the persecutor himself inasmuch as his brain was paralysed by the heat of the sun. What was to be brought to an issue in this fight originated in a still earlier incarnation when this individuality had been brilliantly, outstandingly clever. The opponent whom he encountered during the Crusades had suffered injury and embarrassment in an earlier incarnation at the hands of this brilliant individuality. As you see, it all leads back to the moral life, for the forces in play originated in the earlier incarnation.

151

Thus we have three consecutive incarnations of an individuality. A remarkably clever and able personality in very ancient times—that is one incarnation. Following that, a Crusader, who at a certain time in his life gets paralysis of the brain, brought about as the result of a wrong committed by his cleverness which had, however, in the next incarnation, caused him to acquire tremendous admiration for oriental civilisation. Third incarnation: a Prussian officer who is obliged to retire owing to an affliction of the knee, does not know what to do with his time, goes in for philosophy and writes a most impressive book, a perfect product of the civilisation of the second half of the 19th century: *The Philosophy of the Unconscious.*

Once this connection of lives is perceived, things that were previously obscure become quite clear. When I was reading Hartmann while I was still young, without knowing anything about these connections, I always had the feeling: Yes, this is extremely clever! But when I had read one page I used to think: There is something brilliantly clever here, but the cleverness is not on this particular page! I always felt I must turn the page and look at the previous one to see if the cleverness were there. In short, the cleverness in this writing was not of to-day, but of yesterday, or of the day before yesterday.

Light came to me for the first time when I perceived: the outstanding cleverness really lies two incarnations ago and is working on from there. Great illumination is shed upon the whole of this Hartmann literature—which, as I said, is a library in itself—as soon as one realises that the cleverness in it is working on from a much earlier incarnation.

And when one came to know Eduard von Hartmann personally and was talking with him, one also felt: another man is there behind him, but even he is not the one who is talking; behind him again is a third, and it is the third who is really the source of the inspirations. For listening to Hartmann was often enough to drive one to despair! There was an officer, talking philosophy without enthusiasm, apathetically, speaking with a certain crudity of the loftiest truths. One could see how things really were only when one knew: the cleverness behind what he says is that of two incarnations ago.

It may seem disrespectful to relate such things, but no disrespect whatever is intended. Moreover I am convinced that it can be of great value for any human being to know of such connections and apply them to his own life, even if it means that he has to say to himself: Three incarnations ago I was an out-and-out scoundrel! It can be of immense benefit to life when a man can say to himself: In one incarnation or another, perhaps not only in one, I was a thoroughly bad lot! In speaking of such things, just as in other circumstances present company is always excepted, so here present incarnations are excepted!

I was also intensely interested in the connections of destiny of a man with whom my own life brought me into contact, namely *Friedrich Nietzsche*. I have studied the problem of Nietzsche in all its aspects and, as you know, have written and spoken a great deal about him.

His was indeed a strange and remarkable destiny. I saw him only once during his life. It was in Naumburg, in the nineties of last century, when his mind was already seriously deranged. In the afternoon, about half-past-two, his sister took me into his room. He lay on the couch, listless and unresponsive, with eyes unable to see that someone was standing by him: He lay there with the remarkable, beautifully formed brow that made such a striking impression upon one. Although the eyes were expressionless, one nevertheless had the feeling: This is not a case of insanity, but rather of a man who has been working spiritually the whole morning with great intensity of soul, has had his mid-day meal and is now lying at rest, pondering, half dreamily pondering on what his soul worked out in the morning. Spiritually seen, there were present only a physical body and an etheric body, especially in respect of the upper parts of the organism, for the being of soul-and-spirit was already outside, attached to the body as it were by a stubborn thread only. In reality a kind of death had already set in, but a death that could not be complete because the physical organisation was so healthy.

153

The astral body and the ego that would fain escape were still held by the extraordinarily healthy metabolic and rhythmic organisations, while a completely ruined nerves-and-senses system was no longer able to hold the astral body and the ego. So one had the wonderful impression that the true Nietzsche was hovering above the head. There he was. And down below was something that from the vantage-point of the soul might well have been a corpse, and was only not a corpse because it still held on with might and main to the soul—but only in respect of the lower parts of the organism— because of the extraordinarily healthy metabolic and rhythmic organisation.

Such a spectacle may well make one attentive to the connections of destiny. In this case, at any rate, quite a different light was thrown upon them. Here one could not start from a suffering limb or the like, but one was led to look at the spirituality of Friedrich Nietzsche in its totality.

There are three strongly marked and distinct periods in Nietzsche's life. The first period begins when he wrote *The Birth of Tragedy out of the Spirit of Music* while he was still quite young, inspired by the thought of music springing from Greek tragedy which had itself been born from music. Then, in the same strain, he wrote the four following works: *David Friedrich Strauss; Confessor and Author, Schopenhauer as Educator, Thoughts out of Season, Richard Wagner in Bayreuth*. This was in the year 1876. (*The Birth of Tragedy* was written in 1871). *Richard Wagner in Bayreuth* is a hymn of praise to Richard Wagner, actually perhaps the best thing that has been written by any admirer of Wagner.

Then a second period begins. Nietzsche writes his books, *Human, All-too Human*, in two volumes, the work entitled *Dawn* and thirdly, *The Joyful Wisdom*.

In the early writings, up to the year 1876, Nietzsche was in the highest sense of the word an idealist. In the second epoch of his life he bids farewell to idealism in every shape and form; he makes fun of ideals; he convinces himself that if men set themselves ideals, this is due to weakness. When a man can do nothing in life, he says: Life is not worth any-

154

thing, one must hunt for an ideal.—And so Nietzsche knocks down ideals one by one, puts them to the test, and conceives the manifestations of the Divine in nature as something " all-too-human," something paltry and petty. Here we have Nietzsche the disciple of Voltaire, to whom he dedicates one of his writings. Nietzsche is here the rationalist, the intellectualist. And this phase lasts until about the year 1882 or 1883. Then begins the final epoch of his life, when he unfolds ideas like that of the Eternal Recurrence and presents the figure of Zarathustra as a human ideal. He writes *Thus spake Zarathustra* in the style of a hymn.

Then he takes out again the notes he had once made on Wagner, and here we find something very remarkable! If one follows Nietzsche's way of working, it does indeed seem strange. Read his work *Richard Wagner in Bayreuth.*—It is a grand, enraptured hymn of praise. And now, in the last epoch of his life, comes the book *The Case of Wagner*, in which everything that can possibly be said against Wagner is set down!

If one is content with trivialities, one will simply say: Nietzsche has changed sides, he has altered his views. But those who are really familiar with Nietzsche's manuscripts will not speak in this way. In point of fact, when Nietzsche had written a few pages in the form of a hymn of praise to Wagner, he then proceeded to write down as well everything he could against what he himself had said! Then he wrote another hymn of praise, and then again he wrote in the reverse sense! The whole of *The Case of Wagner* was actually written in 1876, only Nietzsche put it aside, discarded it, and printed only the hymn of praise. And all that he did later on was to take his old drafts and interpolate a few caustic passages.

In this last period of his life the urge came to him to carry through an attack which in the first epoch he had abandoned. In all probability, if the manuscript he put aside as being out of keeping with his *Richard Wagner in Bayreuth* had been destroyed by fire, we should never have had *The Case of Wagner* at all.

If you study these three periods in Nietzsche's life you will find that all show evidence of a uniform trend. Even the last book, the last published writing at any rate, *The Twilight of Idols*, which shows entirely his other side—even this last book bears something of the fundamental character of Nietzsche's spiritual life. In old age, however, when this work was composed, he becomes imaginative, writing in a graphic, vividly descriptive style. For example, he wants to characterise Michelet, the French writer. He lights on a very apt expression when he speaks of him as having the kind of enthusiasm that takes off its coat. This is a marvellously apt description of one aspect of Michelet. Other similar utterances—graphic and imaginative—are also to be found in *The Twilight of Idols*.

If you once have this tragic, deeply moving picture before you of the individuality hovering above the body of Nietzsche, you will be compelled to say of his writings that the impression they make is as though Nietzsche were never fully present in his body while he was writing down his sentences. He used to write, you know, sometimes sitting but more often while walking, especially while going for long tramps. It is as though he had always been a little outside his body. You will have this impression most strongly of all in the case of certain passages in the fourth part of *Thus Spake Zarathustra*, of which you will feel that they could have been written only when the body no longer had control, when the soul was outside the body.

One feels that when Nietzsche is being spiritually creative, he always leaves his body behind. And this same tendency can be perceived, too, in his habits. He was particularly fond of taking chloral in order to induce a mood that strives to get away from the body, a mood of aloofness from the body. This tendency was of course due to the fact that the body was in many respects ailing; for example, Nietesche suffered from constant and always very prolonged headaches, and so on.

All these things give a uniform picture of Nietzsche in this incarnation at the end of the 19th century, an incarnation which finally culminated in insanity, so that he no longer knew who he was. There are letters addressed to George Brandes signed "The Crucified One"—indicating that Nietzsche regards himself as the Crucified One; and at another time he looks at himself as at a man who is actually present outside him, thinks that he is a God walking by the River Po, and signs himself "Dionysos." This separation from the body while spiritual work is going on reveals itself as something that is peculiarly characteristic of this personality, characteristic, that is to say, of this particular incarnation.

If we ponder this inwardly, with Imagination, then we are led back to an incarnation lying not so very long ago. It is characteristic of many such representative personalities that their previous incarnations do not lie in the distant past but in the comparatively near past, even, maybe, in quite recent times.

We come to a life where this individuality was a Franciscan, a Franciscan ascetic who inflicted intense self-torture on his body. Now we have the key to the riddle. The gaze falls upon a man in the characteristic Franciscan habit, lying for hours at a time in front of the altar, praying until his knees are bruised and sore, beseeching grace, mortifying his flesh with severest penances—with the result that through the self-inflicted pain he knits himself very strongly with his physical body. Pain makes one intensely aware of the physical body because the astral body yearns after the body that is in pain, wants to penetrate it through and through. The effect of this concentration upon making the body fit for salvation in the one incarnation was that, in the next, the soul had no desire to be in the body at all.

Such are the connections of destiny in certain typical cases. It can certainly be said that they are not what one would have expected! In the matter of successive earthly lives, speculation is impermissible and generally leads to false conclusions. But when we do come upon the truth, marvellous enlightenment is shed upon life.

Because studies of this kind can help us to look at karma

in the right way, I have not been afraid—although such a course has its dangers—to give you certain concrete examples of karmic connections which can, I think, throw a great deal of light upon the nature of human karma, of human destiny.

X

In our study of karmic connections I have hitherto followed the practice of starting from personalities in more recent times and then going back to their previous lives on earth. To-day, in order to amplify the actual examples of karmic connections, I propose to go the other way, starting from certain personalities of the past and following them into later times, either into some later epoch of history, or right into the life of the present day. What I want to do is to give you a picture of certain historic connections, presenting it in such a way that at every point some light is shed on the workings of karma.

If you follow the development of Christianity from its foundation, tracing the various paths taken by the Christian Impulse on its way across Europe, you will encounter a different stream of spiritual life which, although little heed is paid to it to-day, exercised an extraordinarily deep influence upon European civilisation under the surface of external events. It is the stream known as Mohammedanism, the Mohammedan religion, which, as you know, came into existence rather more than 500 years after the founding of Christianity, together with the mode of life associated with it.

We see, in the first place, that monotheism in a very strict form was instituted by Mohammed. It is a religion that looks up, as did Judaism, to a single Godhead encompassing the universe. "There is one God and Mohammed is his herald."—That is what goes forth from Arabia as a mighty impulse, spreading far into Asia, passing across Africa and thence into Europe by way of Spain.

Anyone who studies the civilisation of our own time will misjudge many things if he ignores the influences which, having received their initial impetus from the deed of

Mohammed, penetrated into European civilisation as the result of the Arabian campaigns, although the actual form of religious feeling with which these influences were associated did not make its way into Europe.

When we consider the form in which Mohammedanism made its appearance, we find, first and foremost, the uncompromising monotheism, the one, all-powerful Godhead —a conception of Divinity that is allied with fatalism. The destiny of man is predetermined; he must submit to this destiny, or at least recognise his subjection to it. This attitude is an integral part of the religious life. But this Arabism—for let us call it so—also brought in its train something entirely different. The strange thing is that while, on the one hand, the warlike methods adopted by Arabism created disturbance and alarm among the peoples, on the other hand it is also remarkable that for well-nigh a thousand years after the founding of Mohammedanism, Arabism did very much to promote and further civilisation. If we look at the period when Charlemagne's influence in Europe was at its prime, we find over in Asia, at the Court in Bagdad, much wonderful culture, a truly great and splendid spiritual life. While Charlemagne was trying to spread an elementary kind of culture on primitive foundations—he himself only learnt to write out of sheer necessity—spiritual culture of a very high order was flourishing over yonder in Asia, in Bagdad. Moreover, this spiritual culture inspired tremendous respect in the environment of Charles the Great himself.

At the time when Charles the Great was ruling—768 to 814 are the dates given—we see over in Bagdad, in the period from 786 to 809, *Haroun al Raschid* as the figure-head of a civilisation that had achieved great splendour. We see Haroun al Raschid, whose praises have so often been sung by poets, at the centre of a wide circle of activity in the sciences and the arts. He was himself a highly cultured man whose followers were by no means men of such primitive attainments as, for example, Einhard, the associate of Charles the Great. Haroun al Raschid gathered around him men of real brilliance in the field of science and art. We see him in Asia—

not exactly ruling over culture, but certainly giving the impulse to it at a very high level.

And we see how there emerges within this spiritual culture, of which Haroun al Raschid was the soul, something that had been spreading in Asia in a continuous stream since the time of Aristotle. Aristotelian philosophy and natural science had spread across into Asia and had there been elaborated by oriental insight, oriental imagination, oriental vision. Its influence can be traced over the whole of Asia Minor, almost to the frontier of India, and its effectiveness may be judged from the fact that a widespread and highly developed system of medicine, for example, was cultivated at this Court of Haroun al Raschid.

Profound philosophic thought is applied to what had been founded by Mohammed with a kind of religious furore; we see this becoming the object of intense study and being put to splendid application by the scholars, poets, scientists and physicians living at this Court in Bagdad.

Mathematics was cultivated there, also geography. Unfortunately, far too little is heard of this in European history, and the primitive doings at the Frankish Court of Charles the Great are apt to obscure what was being achieved over in Asia.

When we consider all that had developed directly out of Mohammedanism, we have before us a most remarkable picture. Mohammedanism was founded in Mecca and carried further in Medina. It spread into the regions of Damascus, Bagdad and so forth, indeed, over the whole of Asia Minor, exercising the dominating influence I have described. This is the one direction in which Mohammedanism spreads —northwards from Arabia and across Asia Minor. The Arabs continually lay siege to Constantinople. They knock at the doors of Europe. They want to force their way across Eastern Europe towards Middle Europe.

On the other hand, Arabism spreads across the North of Africa and thence into Spain. It takes hold of Europe as it were from the other direction, by way of Spain.

We have before us the remarkable spectacle of Europe

161

tending to be surrounded by Arabism—by a forked stream of Arabic culture.

Christianity, in its Roman form, spreads upwards from Rome, from the South, starting from Greece; this impulse is made manifest later on by Ulfila's translation of the Bible, and so forth. And then, enclosing this European civilisation as it were with two forked arms, we have Mohammedanism. Everything that history tells concerning what was done by Charles the Great to further Christianity must be considered in the light of the fact that while Charles the Great did much to promote Christianity in Middle Europe, at the same time there was flourishing over yonder in Asia that illustrious centre of culture of which I have spoken, the centre of culture around Haroun al Raschid.

When we look at the purely external course of history, what do we find ? Wars are waged all along a line stretching across North Africa to the Iberian Peninsula; the followers of Arabism come right across Spain and are beaten back by the representatives of European Christianity, by Charles Martel, by Charles the Great himself. Then, later, we find how the greatness of Mohammedanism is overclouded by the Turkish element which assumes the guise of religion but extinguishes everything that went with the lofty culture to which Haroun al Raschid gave the impetus.

These two streams gradually die out as a result of the struggle waged against them by the warlike Christian population of Europe. Towards the end of the first thousand years, the only real menace in Europe comes from the Turks, but this has nothing much to do with what we are here considering. From now onwards no more is to be heard of the spread of Arabism.

Observation of history in its purely external aspect might lead us to the conclusion that Arabism had been beaten back by the European peoples. Battles were fought such as that of Tours and Poitiers, and there were many others; the Arabs were also defeated from the side of Constantinople, and it might easily be thought that Arabism had disappeared from the arena of world-history.

162

On the other hand, when we think deeply about the impulses that were at work in the sciences, and also in many respects in the field of art in European culture, we find Arabism still in evidence—but as if it had secretly poured into Christianity, had been secretly inculcated into it.

How has this come about ? You must realise, my dear friends, that in spiritual life, events do not take the form in which they reveal themselves in external history. The really significant streams run their course *beneath* the surface of ordinary history and in these streams the individualities of the men who have worked in one epoch appear again, born into communities speaking an entirely different language, with altogether different tendencies of thought, yet working still with the same fundamental impulse. In an earlier epoch they may have accomplished something splendid, because the trend of events was with them, while in a later they may have had to bring it into the world in face of great hindrances and obstructions. Such individuals are obliged to content themselves with much that seems trivial in comparison with the mighty achievements of their earlier lives; but for all that, what they carry over from one epoch into another is the same in respect of the fundamental trend and attitude of soul. We do not always recognise what is thus carried over because we are too prone to imagine that a later earthly life must resemble an earlier one. There are people who think that a musician must come again as a musician, a philosopher as a philosopher, a gardener as a gardener, and so forth. By no means is it so. The forces that are carried over from one incarnation into another lie on far deeper levels of the life of soul.

When we perceive this, we realise that Arabism did not, in truth, die out. From the examples of Friedrich Theodor Vischer and of Schubert I was recently able to show you how the work and achievements of individualities in an earlier epoch continue, in a later one, in totally different forms.

Arabism most assuredly did not die out; far rather was it that individuals who were firmly rooted in Arabism lived in European civilisation and influenced it strongly, in a way that was possible in Europe in that later epoch.

Now it is easier to go forward from some historical personality in order to find him again than to go the reverse way, as in recent lectures—starting from later incarnations and then going back to earlier ones. When we learn to know the individuality of Haroun al Raschid inwardly in the astral light, as we say, when we have him before us as a spiritual individuality in the 9th century, bearing in mind what he was behind the scenes of world-history—and when what he was had been unfolded on the surface with the brilliance of which I have told you—then we can follow the course of time and find such an individuality as Haroun al Raschid passing through death, looking down from the spiritual world upon what is happening on earth, looking down, that is to say, upon the outward extermination of Arabism and, in accordance with his destiny, being involved in the process. We find such an individuality passing through the spiritual world and appearing again, not perhaps with the same splendour, but with a similar trend of soul.

And so we see Haroun al Raschid appearing again in the history of European spiritual life as a personality who is once again of wide repute, namely, as *Lord Bacon of Verulam.* I have spoken of Lord Bacon in many different connections. All the driving power that was in Haroun al Raschid and was conveyed to those in his environment, this same impulse was imparted by Lord Bacon in a more abstract form—for he lived in the age of abstraction—to the various branches of knowledge. Haroun al Raschid was a universal spirit in the sense that he united specialists, so to speak, around him. Lord Bacon—he has of course his Inspirer behind him, but he is a fit subject to be so inspired—Lord Bacon is a personality who is also able to exercise a truly universal influence.

When with this knowledge of an historic karmic connection we turn to Bacon and his writings, we recognise why these writings have so little that is Christian about them and such a strong Arabic timbre. We discover the genuine Arabist trend in these writings of Lord Bacon. And many things too in regard to his character, which has been so often impugned, will be explicable when we see in him the reincarnated

Haroun al Raschid. The life and culture pursued at the Court of Haroun al Raschid, and justly admired by Charles the Great himself, become the abstract science of which Lord Bacon was the bearer. But men bowed before Lord Bacon too. And whoever studies the attitude adopted by European civilisation in the 8th/9th centuries to Haroun al Raschid, and then the attitude of European learning to Lord Bacon, will have the impression: men have turned round, that is all! In the days of Haroun al Raschid they looked towards the East; then they turned round in Middle Europe and looked towards the West, to Lord Bacon.

And so what may have disappeared, outwardly speaking, from history, is carried from age to age by human individualities themselves. Arabism seems to have disappeared; but it lives on, lives on in its fundamental trend. And just as the outer aspects of a human life differ from those of the foregoing life, so do the influences exercised by such a personality differ from age to age.

Open your history books, and you will find that the year 711 was of great significance in the situation between Europe and the Arabism that was storming across Spain. Tarik, Commander of the Arabs, sets out from Africa. He comes to the place that received its name from him: Gebel al Tarik, later called Gibraltar. The battle of Jerez de la Frontera takes place in the year 711. Arabism makes a strong thrust across Spain at the beginning of the 8th century. Battles are fought, and the fortunes of war sway hither and thither between the peoples who have come down into Spain to join with the old inhabitants, and the Arabs who are now storming in upon them. Even in those days the " culture," as we would say to-day, of the attacking Arabs, commanded tremendous respect in Spain. Naturally, the Europeans had no desire to subject themselves to the Arabs. But the culture the Arabs brought with them was already in a sense a foreshadowing of what flourished later in such unexampled brilliance under Haroun al Raschid. In a man such as Tarik there was the attitude of soul that in all the storms of war wants to give expression to what is contained in Arabism.

165

What we see outwardly is the tumult of war. But along the paths of these wars comes much lofty culture. Even outwardly a very great deal in the way of art and science was established in Spain. Many remains of Arabism lived on in the spiritual life of Europe. Spain itself soon ceased to play a part in the West of Europe. Nevertheless the fortunes of war swayed to and fro and the fighting continued from Spain; in men such as Spinoza we can see how deep is the influence of Arabist culture. Spinoza cannot be understood unless we see his origin in Arabism.

And then this stream flows across to England, but there it runs dry, comes to an end. We turn over the pages of history, and after the descriptions of the conflicts between Europe and the Arabs we find, as we read on further, that Arabism has dried up, externally at any rate. But under the surface this has not happened; on the contrary, Arabism spreads abroad in the spiritual life. And along this undercurrent of history, Tarik bears what he originally bore into Spain on the fierce wings of war. The aim of the Arabians in their campaigns was most certainly not that of mere slaughter; no, their aim was really the spread of Arabism. Their tasks were connected with culture. And what a Tarik had carried into Spain at the beginning of the 8th century, he now bears with him through the gate of death, experiencing how as far as external history is concerned it runs dry in Western Europe. And he appears again in the 19th century, bringing Arabism to expression in modern form, as *Charles Darwin*.

Suddenly we shall find a light shed upon something that seems to come like a bolt from the blue—we find a light shed upon it when we follow what has here been carried over from an earlier into a later time, appearing in an entirely different form.

It may at first seem like a paradox, but the paradox will disappear the more deeply we look into the concrete facts. Read Darwin's writings again with perception sharpened by what has been said and you will feel: Darwin writes about things which Tarik might have been able to see on his way to Europe!—In such details you will perceive how the one life reaches over into the next.

166

Now from times of hoary antiquity, especially in Asia Minor, astronomy had been the subject of profound study— astronomy, that is to say, in an astrological form. This must not, of course, in any way be identified with the quackery perpetuated in the modern age as astrology. We must realise the deep insight into the spiritual structure of the universe possessed by men in those times; this insight was particularly marked among the Arabians in the period when they were Mohammedans, continuing the dynasty founded by Mohammed. Astrological astronomy in its ancient form was cultivated with great intensity among them.

When the Residence of the dynasty was transferred from Damascus to Bagdad, we find *Mamun* ruling there in the 9th century. During the reign of Mamun—all such rulers were successors of the Prophet—astrology was cultivated in the form in which it afterwards passed over into Europe, contained in tracts and treatises of every variety which were only later discovered. They came over to Europe in the wake of the Crusades but had suffered terribly from erroneous and clumsy revision. For all that, however, this astronomy was great and sublime. And when we search among those who are not named in history, but who were around Mamun in Bagdad in the period from 813 to 833, cultivating this astrological-astronomical knowledge, we find a brilliant personality in whom Mamun placed deep confidence. His name is not given in history, but that is of no account. He was a personality most highly respected, to whom appeal was always made when it was a question of reading the portents of the stars. Many measures connected with the external social life were formulated in accordance with what such celebrities as the learned scholar at the Court of Caliph Mamun were able to read in the stars.

And if we follow the line along which the soul of this learned man at the Court of Mamun in Bagdad developed, we are led to the modern astronomer *Laplace*. Thus one of the personalities who lived at the Court of the Caliph Mamun appears again as Laplace.

The great impulses—those of less importance, too, which

I need not now enumerate—that still flowed from this two-branched stream into Europe, even after the outer process had come to a halt, show us how Arabism lived on spiritually, how this two-pronged fork around Europe continued its grip.

You will remember, my dear friends, that Mohammed himself founded the centre of Mohammedanism, Medina, which later on became the seat of residence of his successors; this seat of residence was subsequently transferred to Damascus. Then, from Damascus across to Asia Minor and to the very portal of Europe, Constantinople, the generals of Mohammed's successors storm forward, again on the wings of war, bearing culture that has been fructified by the religion and the religious life founded by Mohammed, but is permeated also with the *Aristotelianism* which in the wake of the campaigns of Alexander the Great was carried over from Greece, from Macedonia, indeed from many centres of culture, to Asia.

And here, too, something very remarkable happens. Arabism is flooded, swamped, by the Turkish element. The Crusaders find rudimentary relics only, not the fruits of an all-prevailing culture. All this was eliminated by the Turks. What was carried by way of Africa and Spain to the West lives on and develops in the tranquil flow, so to speak, of civilisation and culture; points of contact are again and again to be found.

The unnamed scholar at the Court of Mamun, Haroun al Raschid himself, Tarik—all these souls were able to link what they bore within them with what was actually present in the world. For when the soul has passed through the gate of death, a certain force of attraction to the regions which were the scene of previous activity always remains; even when through other impulses of destiny there may have been changes, nevertheless the influence continues. It works on, maybe in the form of longing or the like. But because Arabism promotes belief in strict determinism, when the opportunity offered for continuing in a spiritual way what, at the beginning, was deliberately propagated by warlike means, it also became possible to carry these spiritual streams especially into France and England. Laplace,

Darwin, Bacon, and many other spirits of like nature were led forward in this direction.

But everything had been, as it were, damped down. In the East, Arabism was able to knock only feebly at the door of Europe; it could make no real progress there. And those who passed through the gate of death after having worked in this region felt repulsed, experienced a sense of inability to go forward. The work they had performed on earth was destroyed, and the consequence of this between death and rebirth was a kind of paralysis of the life of soul.—We come now to something of extraordinary interest.

Soon after the time of the Prophet, the Residence is transferred from Medina to Damascus. From there the generals of the successors of the Prophet go forth with their armies but are again and again beaten back; the success achieved in the West is not achieved here. And then, very soon, we see a successor of the Prophet, Muavija by name, ruling in Damascus. His attitude and constitution of soul proceed on the one side from the monotheism of Arabism, but also from the determinism which grew steadily into fatalism. But already at that time, although in a more inward, mystical way, the Aristotelianism that had been carried over to Asia was taking effect. Muavija, who sent his generals on the one side as far as Constantinople and on the other made attempts—without any success to speak of—in the direction of Africa, this Muavija was at the same time a thoughtful man; but a man who did not accomplish anything very much, either outwardly or in the spiritual life.

Muavija rules not long after Mohammed. He thus stands entirely within Mohammedanism, within the religious life of Arabism. He is a genuine representative of Mohammedanism at that time, but one of those who are growing away from its hide-bound form and entering into that mode of thought which then, discarding the religious form, appears in the sciences and fine arts of the West.

Muavija is a representative spirit in the first century after Mohammed, but one whose thinking is no longer patterned in absolute conformity with that of Mohammed; he draws

169

his impulse from Mohammed, but only his impulse. He has not yet discarded the religious core of Mohammedanism, but has already led it over into the sphere of thought, of logic. And above all he is one of those who are ardently intent upon pressing on into Europe, upon forcing their way to the West. If you follow the campaigns and observe the forces that were put into operation under Muavija, you will realise that this eagerness to push forward towards the West was combined with tremendous driving power, but this was already blunted, was already losing its edge.

When such a spirit later passes through the gate of death and lives on, the driving force also persists, and if we follow the path further we get this striking impression.—During the life between death and a new birth, much that remained as longing is elaborated into world-encompassing plans for a later life, but world-encompassing plans that assume no very concrete form for the very reason that the force behind them was blunted.

Now I confess that I am always having to ask myself: Shall I or shall I not speak openly ? But after all it is useless to speak of these matters merely in abstractions, and so one must lay aside reserve and speak of things that are there in concrete cases. Let the world think as it will: certain inner, spiritual necessities exist in connection with the spread of Anthroposophy. One lends oneself to the impulse that arises from these spiritual necessities, pursuing no outward " opportunism." Opportunism has, in sooth, wrought harm enough to the Anthroposophical Society; in the future there must be no more of it. And even if things have a paradoxical effect, they will henceforward be said straight out.

If we follow this Muavija, one of the earliest successors of the Prophet, as he passes along the undercurrent and then appears again, we find *Woodrow Wilson*.

In a shattering way the present links itself with the past. A bond is suddenly there between present and past. And if we observe how on the sea of historical happenings there surges up as it were the wave of Muavija, and again the wave of Woodrow Wilson, we perceive how the undercurrent flows on through the sea below and appears again—it is the same current.

I believe that history becomes intelligible only when we see how what really happens has been carried over from one epoch into another. Think of the abstraction, the rigid abstraction, of the Fourteen Points. Needless to say, the research did not take its start from the Fourteen Points—but now that the whole setting lies before you, look at the configuration of soul that comes to expression in these Fourteen Points and ask yourselves whether it could have taken root with such strength anywhere else than in a follower of Mohammed.

Take the fatalism that had already assumed such dimensions in Muavija and transfer it into the age of modern abstraction. Feel the similarity with Mohammedan sayings: " Allah has revealed it "; " Allah will bring it to pass as the one and only salvation." And then try to understand the real gist of many a word spoken by the promoter of the Fourteen Points.—With no great stretch of imagination you will find an almost literal conformity.

Thus, when we are observing human beings, we can also speak of a reincarnation of *ideas*. And then for the first time insight is possible into the growth and unfolding of history.

XI

Our studies of karma, which have led us lately to definite individual examples of karmic relationships, are intended to afford a basis for forming a judgment not only of individual human connections, but also of more general historical ones. And it is with this end in view that I would like now to add to the examples already given. To-day we will prepare the ground, and to-morrow we will follow this up by showing the karmic connections.

You will have realised that consideration of the relation between one earth-life and the next must always be based upon certain definite symptoms and facts. If we take these as our starting-point, they will lead us to a view of the actual connections. And in the case of the individualities of whom I have ventured to tell you, I have shown where these particular starting-points are to be found.

To-day I want, as I said, to prepare the way, placing before you problems of which we shall find the solutions to-morrow.

Let me first draw your attention to the peculiar interest that one or another personality can arouse. I shall speak of personalities of historical interest as well as of personalities in ordinary life; the very interest that some persons arouse in us will often urge us to find a clue to their life-connections. Once we know how to look for these clues in the right way, we shall be able to find them. As you will already have noticed from the way in which I have presented the cases, it is all a matter of seeking in the right way. Let us then not be deterred, but proceed boldly.

Whatever one's attitude to the personality of *Garibaldi* may be in other respects, there can be no doubt that he is an interesting figure in the history of Europe; he played, as we all know, a remarkable part in the events of the 19th century.

To-day, then, we will make a preparatory study of Garibaldi, and to begin with I will bring to your notice certain facts in his life which, as we shall find, are able to lead the student of spiritual science to the connections of which we shall learn to-morrow.

Garibaldi is a personality who participated in a remarkable way in the life of the 19th century. He was born in the year 1807 and he held a prominent and influential position on into the second half of the century. This means that the way he expresses himself as a man is highly characteristic of the 19th century.

When we come to consider the features of his life, looking especially for those that are important from a spiritual aspect, we find Garibaldi spending his boyhood in Nice as the son of a poor man who has a job in the navigation service. He is a child who has little inclination to take part in what the current education of the country has to offer, a child who is not at all brilliant at school, but who takes a lively interest in all sorts and varieties of human affairs. What he learns at school has indeed the effect of inducing him very often to play truant. While the teacher was trying in his own way to bring some knowledge of the world to the children, the boy Garibaldi much preferred to romp about out-of-doors, to scamper through the woods or play games by the riverside. On the other hand, if he once got hold of some book that appealed to him, nothing could tear him from it. He would lie on his back by the hour in the sunshine, absolutely absorbed, not even going home for meals.

Broadly speaking, however, it was the great world that interested him. While still quite young he set about preparing himself for his father's calling and took part in sea voyages, at first in a subordinate, and afterwards in an independent position. He made many voyages on the Adriatic and shared in all the varied experiences that were to be had in the first half of the 19th century, when Liberalism and Democracy had not yet organised the traffic on the sea and put it under police regulations, but when some freedom of movement was still left in the life of man! He shared in

174

all the experiences that were possible in times when one could do more or less what one wanted! And so he also had the experience—I believe it happened to him three or four times —of being seized by pirates. As well as being a genius, however, he was sly, and every time he was caught, he got away again, and very quickly too!

And so Garibaldi grew up into manhood, always living in the great world. As I have said, I do not intend to give you a biography but to point out characteristic features of his life that can lead us on to a consideration of what is really important and essential. He lived in the great world, and there came a time when he acquired a very strong and vivid impression of what his own inner relationship to the world might be. It was when he was nearly grown up and was taken by his father on a journey through the country, as far as Rome. There, looking out from Rome as it were over all Italy, he must have been aware of something quite remarkable going through his soul. In his voyages he had met many people who were, in general, quite alive and awake, but were utterly indifferent to one particular interest—they were asleep as regards the conditions of the time; and these people made an impression on Garibaldi that nearly drove him to despair. They had no enthusiasm for true and genuine humanity, such as showed itself in him quite early in life—he had indeed a genius for warm, tender-hearted enthusiasm.

As he passed through the countryside and afterwards came to Rome, a kind of vision must have arisen in his soul of the part he was later to play in the liberation of Italy. Other circumstances also helped to make him a fanatical anti-cleric, and a fanatical Republican, a man who set clearly before him the aim of doing everything in his power to further the well-being of mankind.

And now, taking part as he did in all manner of movements in Italy in the first half of the 19th century, it happened one day that for the first time in his life, Garibaldi read his name in the newspaper. I think he was about thirty years old at the time. It meant a good deal more in those days than it would do now, to read one's name in the newspaper. Garibaldi had, however, a peculiar destiny in connection with this reading of his name in the newspaper, for the occasion was the announcement in the paper of his death-sentence! He read his name there for the first time when his sentence to death was reported. There you have a unique circumstance of his life; it is not every man who has such an experience.

It was not granted to Garibaldi—and it is characteristic of his destiny that it was not, considering that his whole enthusiasm was centred in Italy—it was not granted him at first to take a hand in the affairs of Italy or Europe, but it was laid upon him by destiny to go first to South America and take part in all manner of movements for freedom over there, until the year 1848. And in every situation he showed himself a most remarkable man, gifted with quite extraordinary qualities. I have already related to you one most singular event in his life, the finding of his name in the newspaper for the first time on the occasion of the announcement of his own death-sentence. And now we come to another quite individual biographical fact, something that happens to very few men indeed. Garibaldi became acquainted in a most extraordinary way with the woman who was to be the mainstay of his happiness for many years. He was out at sea, on board ship, looking landwards through a telescope. To fall in love through a telescope—that is certainly not the way it happens to most people!

Destiny again made it easy for him to become quickly acquainted with the one whom he had chosen through the telescope to be his beloved. He steered at once in the direction in which he had looked through the telescope, and on reaching land he was invited by a man to a meal. It transpired, after he had accepted the invitation, that this man was the father of the girl he had seen! She could speak only Portuguese, and he only Italian; but we are assured by his biographer, and it seems to be correct, that the young woman immediately understood his carefully phrased declaration of love, which seems to have consisted simply of the words—in Italian of course—" We must unite for life."

176

She understood immediately. And it really happened so, that from this meeting came a life-companionship that lasted for a long, long time.

Garibaldi's wife shared in all the terrible and adventurous journeys he made in South America, and some of the recorded details of them are really most moving. For example, the story is told of how a report got about that Garibaldi had been killed in battle. His wife hurried to the battlefield and lifted up every head to see if it were her husband's. After a long time, and after undergoing many adventures in the search, she found him still alive. It is most affecting to read how on this very journey, which lasted a long time, she gave birth to a child without help of any kind, and how, in order to keep it warm, she bound it in a sling about her neck, holding it against her breast for hours at a time. The story of Garibaldi's South American adventures has some deeply moving aspects.

But now the time came, in the middle of the 19th century, when all kinds of impulses for freedom were stirring among the peoples of Europe, and Garibaldi could not bring himself to stay away any longer in South America; he returned to his fatherland. It is well-known with what intense energy he worked there, mustering volunteers under the most difficult circumstances—so much so that he did not merely contribute to the development of the new Italy: he was its creator.

And here we come to a feature of his life and character that stands out very strongly. He was, in every relationship of life, a man of *independence*, a man who always thought in a large and simple way, and took account only of the impulses that welled up from the depths of his own inner being. And so it is really very remarkable to see him doing everything in his power to bring it about that the dynasty of Victor Emmanuel should rule over the kingdom of Italy, when in reality the whole unification and liberation of Italy was due to Garibaldi himself. The story of how he won Naples and then Sicily with, comparatively speaking, quite a small force of men, undisciplined yet filled with enthusiasm, of how the future King of Italy needed only to make his entry into the

177

regions already won for him by Garibaldi, and of how, nevertheless, if truth be told, nothing whatever was done from the side of the royal family or of those who stood near to them to show any proper appreciation of what Garibaldi had accomplished—the whole story makes a deep and striking impression. Fundamentally speaking, if we may put it in somewhat trivial language, the Savoy Dynasty had Garibaldi to thank for everything, and yet they were eminently unthankful to him, treating him with no more than necessary politeness.

Take, for example, the entry into Naples. Garibaldi had won Naples for the Dynasty and was regarded by the Neapolitans as no less than their liberator; a perfect storm of jubilation always greeted his appearance. It would have been unthinkable for the future King of Italy to make his entry into Naples without Garibaldi, absolutely unthinkable. Nevertheless the King's advisers were against it. Advisers, no doubt, are often exceedingly short-sighted; but if Victor Emmanuel had not acted on his own account out of a certain instinct and made Garibaldi sit by him in his red shirt on the occasion of the entry into Naples, he himself would most certainly not have been greeted with shouts of rejoicing! Even so, the cheers were intended for Garibaldi and not for him. He would most assuredly have been hissed—that is an absolute certainty. Victor Emmanuel would have been hissed if he had entered Naples without Garibaldi.

And it was the same all through. At some campaign or other in the centre of Italy, Garibaldi had carried the day. The commanders-in-chief with the King had come—what does one say in such a case, putting it as kindly as one can? —they had come too late. The whole thing had been carried through to the finish by Garibaldi. When, however, the army appeared, with its generals wearing their decorations, and met Garibaldi's men who had no decorations and were moreover quite unpretentiously attired, the generals declared: It is beneath our dignity to ride side by side with them, we cannot possibly do such a thing! But Victor Emmanuel had some sort of instinct in these matters. He called Garibaldi

to his side, and the generals, making wry faces, were obliged
to join with Garibaldi's army as it drew up into line. These
generals, it seems, had a terribly bad time of it; they looked as
though they had stomach-aches! And afterwards, when the
entry into a town was to be made, Garibaldi, who had done
everything, actually had to come on behind like a rearguard.
He and his men had to wait and let the others march in front.
It was a case where the regular army had in point of fact done
absolutely nothing; yet they entered first, and after them,
Garibaldi with his followers.

The important things to note are these remarkable links of
destiny. It is in these links of destiny that we may find our
guidance to the karmic connections. For it has not directly
to do with a man's freedom or unfreedom that he first sees
his name in print on the occasion of his death-sentence, or
that he finds his wife through a telescope. Such things are
connections of destiny; they take their course alongside of
that which is always present in man in spite of them—his
freedom. These are the very things, however—these things
of which we may be sure that they are links of destiny—that
can give a great stimulus to the practical study of the nature
and reality of karma.

Now in the case of a personality like Garibaldi, traits that
may generally be thought incidental, are characteristic. They
are, in his case, strongly marked. Garibaldi was what is
called a handsome man. He had beautiful tawny-golden
hair and was altogether a splendid figure. His hair was curly
and gleaming gold, and was greatly admired by the women!
Now you will agree, from what I have told you of Garibaldi's
bride—whom he chose, you remember, through a telescope—
that only the highest possible praise can be spoken of her;
nevertheless, it seems she was not altogether free from
jealousy. What does Garibaldi do one day when this
jealousy seems to have assumed somewhat large proportions?
He has his beautiful hair all cut away to the roots; he lets
himself be made bald. That was when they were still in
South America. All these things are traits that serve to
show how the necessities of destiny are placed into life.

Garibaldi became, as we know, one of the great men of Europe after his achievements in Italy, and travelling through Italy to-day you know how, from town to town, you pass from one Garibaldi memorial to another. But there have been times when not only in Italy but everywhere in Europe the name of Garibaldi was spoken with the keenest interest and the deepest devotion, when even the ladies in Cologne, in Mainz and in many another place wore blouses in Garibaldi's honour—not to mention London, where Garibaldi's red blouse became quite the fashion.

During the Franco-Prussian War, in 1870, Garibaldi, now an old man, put himself at the disposal of the French, and an interesting incident took place. His only experience, as we know, had been volunteer fighting, such as he had conducted in Italy and also in South America, yet on a certain occasion in this full-scale war he was the one to capture a German flag from under a pile of men who were trying to protect it with their bodies. Garibaldi captured this flag. But he had such respect for the men who had hurled themselves upon the flag to guard it with their own bodies, that he sent it back to its owners. Strange to relate, however, when he appeared in a meeting at some place or other soon afterwards, he was received with hisses on account of what he had done.

You will agree—this is not merely an interesting life, but the life of a man who in very deed and fact is lifted right above all other greatness in evidence in the 19th century! A most remarkable man—so original, so elementary, acting so evidently out of primitive impulses, and at the same time with such genius! Others working with him may perhaps have been better at leading large armies and doing things in an orderly way, but none of them in that deeply materialistic period had such genuine, spontaneous enthusiasm for what they were aiming at.

Here, then, is one of the personalities whom I would like to place before you. As I said, I shall give preparatory descriptions to-day, and to-morrow we will look for the answers.

Another personality, very well-known to you by name, is

180

of exceptional interest in connection with investigations into karma. It is *Lessing*.

The circumstances of Lessing's life, I may say, have always interested me to an extraordinary degree. Lessing is really the founder of the better sort of journalism, the journalism that has substance and is really out to accomplish something. Before Lessing, poets and dramatists had taken their subjects from the aristocracy. Lessing, on the other hand, is at pains to introduce bourgeois life, ordinary middle-class life, into the drama, the life concerned generally with the destinies of men *as men*, and not with the destinies of men in so far as they hold some position in society or the like. Purely human conflicts—that is what Lessing wanted to portray on the stage. In the course of his work he applied himself to many great problems, as for example when he tried to determine the boundaries of painting and of poetry in his *Laocoon*. But the most interesting thing of all is the powerful impetus with which Lessing fought for the idea of tolerance. You need only take his *Nathan the Wise* and you will see at once what a foremost place this idea of tolerance has in Lessing's mind and life. In weaving the fable of the three kings in *Nathan the Wise*, he wants to show how the three main religions have gone astray from their original forms and are none of them really genuine, and how one must go in search of the true form, which has been lost. Here we have tolerance united with an uncommonly deep and significant idea.

Interesting, too, is the conversation between Freemasons, entitled *Ernst und Falk*, and much else that springs from Freemasonry. What Lessing accomplished in the way of critical research into the history of religious life is, for one who is able to judge its significance, really astounding. But we must be able to place the whole Lessing, in his complete personality, before us. And this we cannot do by reading, for example, the two-volume work by Erich Schmidt which purports to be a final and complete study of Lessing. Lessing as he really was, is not portrayed at all, but a picture is given of a puppet composed of various limbs and members, and we are told that this puppet wrote *Nathan the Wise* and *Laocoon*. It amounts to no more than an assertion that the man portrayed here has written these books. And it is the same with the other biographies of Lessing.

We begin to get an impression of Lessing when we observe, shall I say, the driving force with which he hurls his sentences against his opponents. He wages a polemic against the civilisation of Middle Europe—quite a refined and correct polemic, but at every turn hitting straight home. You must here observe a peculiar nuance in Lessing's character if you want to understand the make-up of his life. On the one hand we have the sharpness, often caustic sharpness, in such writings as *The Dramatic Art of Hamburg*, and then we have to find the way over, as it were, to an understanding, for example, of the words used by Lessing when a son had been born to him and had died directly after birth. He writes somewhat as follows in a letter: Yes, he has at once taken leave again of this world of sorrow; he has thereby done the best thing a human being can do. (I cannot cite the passage word for word, but it was to this effect.) In so writing, Lessing is giving expression to his pain in a wonderfully brave way, not for that reason feeling the pain one whit less deeply than someone who can do nothing but bemoan the event. This ability to draw back into himself in pain was characteristic of the man who at the same time knew how to thrust forward with vigour when he was developing his polemics. This is what makes it so affecting to read the letter written when his child had died immediately after birth, leaving the mother seriously ill.

Lessing had moreover this remarkable thing in his destiny —and it is quite characteristic, when one sets out to find the karmic connections in his case—that he was friends in Berlin with a man who was in every particular his opposite, namely, Nikolai.

Of Lessing it can be said—it is not literally true, but it is none the less characteristic—that he never dreamed, because his intellect and his understanding were so keen. On this account, as we shall see to-morrow, he is for the spiritual researcher such an extraordinarily significant personality. But there is something in the very construction of his sentences, something in the home-thrusts with which he lays his opponent in the dust, that really makes every sentence a delight to read.

With Nikolai it is just the opposite. Nikolai is an example of a true philistine. Although a friend of Lessing, he was none the less a typical philistine-bourgeois; and he had visions, most strange and remarkable visions.

Lessing, genius as he was, had no visions, not even dreams. Nikolai literally *suffered* from visions. They came, and they went away only after leeches had been applied. Yes, in extremity they actually applied leeches to him, in order that he might not be for ever tormented by the spiritual world which would not let him alone.

Fichte wrote a very interesting essay directed against Nikolai. He set out to give a picture of the typical German-bourgeois as shown in the personality of Nikolai. For all that, this same Nikolai was the friend of Lessing.

Another thing is very remarkable in Lessing. In his own *Weltanschauung*, Lessing concerned himself very much with two philosophers, Spinoza and Leibniz. Now it has often attracted me very much, as an interesting occupation for spare hours, to read all the writings in which it is proved over and over again that Lessing was a Leibnizian, and on the other hand those in which it is proved on still more solid ground that he was a Spinozist. For in truth one cannot decide whether Lessing, acute and discerning thinker as he was, was a Leibnizian or a Spinozist, who are the very opposite of each other. Spinoza—pantheist and monotheist; Leibniz—monadist, purely and completely individualistic. And yet we cannot decide whether Lessing belongs to Leibniz or to Spinoza. When we try to put him to the test in this matter, we can come to no conclusive judgment. It is impossible.

At the close of his life Lessing wrote the remarkable essay, *The Education of the Human Race*, at the end of which, quite isolated, as it were, the idea of repeated earth-lives appears.

The book shows how mankind goes through one epoch of development after another, and how the Gods gave into man's hand as a first primer, so to speak, the Old Testament, and then as a second primer the New Testament, and how in the future a third book will come for the further education of the human race. And then all at once the essay is brought to a close with a brief presentation of the idea that man lives through repeated earth-lives. And there Lessing says, again in a way that is absolutely in accord with his character (I am not quoting the actual words, but this is the gist of it): Ought the idea of repeated earth-lives to seem so absurd, considering that it was present in very early times, when men had not yet been spoilt by school learning? The essay then ends with a genuine panegyric on repeated earth-lives, finishing with these beautiful words: " Is not all Eternity mine ? "

One used to meet continually—perhaps it would still be so if one mixed more with people—one used to meet men who valued Lessing highly, but who turned away, so to speak, when they came to *The Education of the Human Race*. Really it is hard to understand the state of mind of such men. They set the highest estimation on a man of genius, and then reject what he gives to mankind in his most mature age. They say: he has grown old, he is senile, we can no longer follow him. That is all very well; one can reject anything by that method! The fact is, no one has any right to recognise Lessing and not to recognise that this work was conceived by him in the full maturity of his powers. When a man like Lessing utters a profound aphorism such as this on repeated earth-lives, there is, properly speaking, no possibility of ignoring it.

You will readily see that the personality of Lessing is interesting in the highest degree from a karmic point of view, in relation to his own passage through different earth-lives. In the second half of the 18th century the idea of repeated earth-lives was by no means a commonly accepted one. It comes forth in Lessing like a flash of lightning, like a flash of genius. We cannot account for its appearance; it cannot possibly be due to Lessing's education or to any other influence in this particular life. We are compelled to ask how it may be with the previous life of a man in whom at a certain age the idea of repeated earth-lives suddenly emerges —an idea that is foreign to the civilisation of his own day— emerges, too, in such a way that the man himself points to the fact that the idea was once present in very early times. The truth is that he is really bringing forward *inner grounds* for the idea, grounds of *feeling* that carry with them an indication of his own earth-life in the distant past. Needless to say, in his ordinary surface-consciousness he has no notion of such connections. The things we do not know are, however, none the less true. If those things alone were true that many men know, then the world would be poor indeed in events and poor indeed in beings.

This is the second case whose karmic connections we are going to study.

There is a third case I should like to open up, because it is one that can teach us a great deal in the matter of karmic relationships. Among the personalities who were near to me as teachers in my youth there was a man to whom I have already referred; to-day I should like to speak of him again, adding some points that will be significant for our study of karma.

There are, of course, risks in speaking of these matters, but in view of the whole situation of the spiritual life which ought to proceed from Anthroposophy to-day, I do not think such risks can be avoided.

What I am now going to tell you came to my notice several years after I had last seen the person in question, who was a greatly beloved teacher of mine up to my eighteenth year. But I had always continued to follow his life, and had in truth remained very close to him. And now at a certain moment in my own life I felt constrained to follow his life more closely in a particular respect.

It was when, in another connection, I began to take a special interest in the life of *Lord Byron*. And at that same time I got to know some Byron enthusiasts. One of them was the poetess, Marie Eugenie delle Grazie, of whom I shall

185

have much to say in my autobiography. During a certain period of her life she was a Byron enthusiast. Then there was another, a most remarkable personality, a strange mixture of all possible qualities—Eugen Heinrich Schmidt. Many of you who know something about the history of Anthroposophy will be familiar with his name.

Eugen Heinrich Schmidt first became known in Vienna during the eighties, and it was then that I made his acquaintance. He had just written the prize essay that was published by the Hegel Society of Berlin, on the Dialectics of Hegel. Now he came to Vienna, a tall, slight man filled with a burning enthusiasm, which came to expression at times in very forcible gestures and so on. It was none the less genuine for that. And it was just this enthusiasm of Schmidt's that gave me the required " jerk," as it were. I thought I would like to do him a kindness, and as he had recently written a most enthusiastic and inspired article on Lord Byron, I introduced him to my other Byron enthusiast, Marie Eugenie delle Grazie. And now began a wildly excited discussion on Byron. The two were really quite in agreement, but they carried on a most lively and animated debate. All we others who were sitting round—a whole collection of theological students from the Vienna Catholic Faculty were there, who came every week and with whom I had made friends—all we others were silent. And the two who were thus conversing about Byron were sitting like this.—Here was the table, rather a long one, and at one end sat delle Grazie and at the other end, Eugen Heinrich Schmidt, gesticulating with might and main. All of a sudden his chair slips away from under him, and he falls under the table, his feet stretching right out to delle Grazie. I can tell you, it was a shock for us all! But this shock helped me to hit upon the solution of a particular problem.

Let me tell you of it quite objectively, as a matter of history. All that they had been saying about Byron had made a strong impression upon me, and I began to feel the keenest need to know how the karmic connections might be in the case of Byron. It was, of course, not so easy. But now I

suddenly had the following experience.—It was really as if the whole picture of this conversation, with Eugen Heinrich Schmidt being so terribly impolite with his foot!—as if this picture had suddenly drawn my attention to the foot of Lord Byron, who was, as you know, club-footed. And from that I went on to say to myself: My beloved teacher, too, had a foot like that; this karmic connection must be investigated. I have already given you an example, in the affliction of the knee from which Eduard von Hartmann suffered, of how one's search can be led back through peculiarities of this kind. I was able now to perceive the destiny of the teacher whom I loved and who also had such a foot. And it was remarkable in the highest degree to observe how on the one hand the same peculiarity came to view both in the case of Byron and of my teacher, namely, the club-foot; but how on the other hand the two persons were totally different from one another, Byron, the poet of genius, who in spite of his genius—or perhaps because of it—was an adventurer; and the other a brilliant geometrician such as one seldom finds in teaching posts, a man at whose geometrical imagination and treatment of descriptive geometry one could only stand amazed.

In short, having before me these two men, utterly different in soul, I was able to solve the problem of their karma by reference to this seemingly insignificant physical detail. This detail it was that enabled me to consider the problems of Byron and my geometry teacher *in connection with one another*, and thereby to find the solution.

I wished to give these examples to-day and to-morrow we will consider them from the point of view of karma.

XII

Yesterday I gave you pictures of two or three personalities. In order to allow for the possibility of proof and confirmation, at least as far as external details are concerned, it is necessary to choose fairly well-known personalities and in describing them to you I have pointed in each case to characteristic qualities which can afford clues for the spiritual scientific investigator and help him to follow up the karmic relationships. This time I have chosen subjects which will also enable me to deal with a problem that has been put to me by members of our Society. Simply stated, it is as follows. Constantly, on every suitable occasion, reference is made—and of course correctly—to the fact that in very early times there were Initiates possessed of a lofty wisdom and at a high stage of development, and the question arises: If human beings pass through repeated earth-lives, where are these highly-initiated personalities ? Where are they to-day ? Are they to be found among the human beings who have been led to reincarnation at the present time ? I have accordingly chosen examples which will enable me to deal with this very problem.

I gave you, as far as was necessary, a picture of the hero of the freedom of Italy, Garibaldi; and if you take what I said yesterday and add to it all that is well-known to you about this personality—a whole wealth of information is available about him—I think you will still find a very great deal in Garibaldi that is puzzling and that opens up significant questions.

Take two events of his life which amused you yesterday.— He became acquainted through a telescope with the girl who was to be his life-companion for many years, and he learnt of his own death-sentence when reading his name for the first time in print. There is still another very striking event in his life. The life-companion whom he found in the way I have described, and who stood at his side with such heroism, was the sharer of his life for many years. He certainly managed to see something very good through his telescope! Later, she died, leaving him alone, and he married a second time, this time not through a telescope—not even a Garibaldi is likely to do such a thing more than once!—this time he married, shall I say, in a perfectly conventional bourgeois manner. But for Garibaldi the marriage lasted no longer than one day. So you see, there is this other very striking fact in Garibaldi's relations with the ordinary bourgeois conditions of this world.

And now we come to something else of importance. The things I am describing to you come, as it were, with a sudden jerk to one accustomed to occult researches of this kind; they are clues that enable his vision to penetrate right into an earlier life or into a number of earlier lives. And in Garibaldi's life there is still another circumstance which raises a formidable problem.

Garibaldi, you know, was a Republican in his very bones; he was a Republican through and through. I made that abundantly clear in yesterday's lecture. And yet in all his plans for the liberation of Italy he never set out to make Italy into a *Republic*, but rather into an *Empire* under Victor Emanuel. That is an astonishing fact. When one looks at Garibaldi's whole life and character and then considers this fact, it really does astonish one.

There we have on the one hand Victor Emmanuel, who could of course reign as king only over a liberated Italy. And we have on the other hand Mazzini—also deeply united in friendship with Garibaldi—who, as you know, stood for a long time at the head of what was intended to be an Italian *Republic*, for he was willing to come forward only as the founder of an Italian Republic. The karmic relationships of Garibaldi will never be solved unless we take note here of a special set of circumstances.

In the course of a few years—Garibaldi, you know, was born at Nice in 1807—there were born within an area of a

comparatively few square miles, four men who had a significant connection with one another in the wider course of
European circumstances. In Nice, at the beginning of the
19th century, Garibaldi was born; in Genoa, not far away,
Mazzini; in Turin, again not far away, Cavour; and from
the House of Savoy, once more at no great distance, Victor
Emanuel. These four men are all quite near to one another
in respect of the times and places of their births. And it is
these four men together who, if not agreeing in thought, if
not even acting always in mutual agreement, nevertheless
established the country which became modern Italy.

You can see how the very way in which these four personalities are brought together in history suggests that they
have, not only for themselves, but for the world, a common
destiny. The most significant among them is, without doubt,
Garibaldi himself. Taking into consideration all human
conditions and relationships, we cannot but agree that he is
by far the most significant figure of the four. Garibaldi's
mentality, however, expresses itself in an elemental way.
Mazzini's mentality is that of a learned philosopher;
Cavour's that of a learned lawyer. And as for Victor Emmanuel's mentality . . . well, there is no doubt about it, the
most important among them all is Garibaldi. He possesses
a quality of mind and spirit that expresses itself with elemental
force, so that one cannot remain indifferent towards it. One
cannot remain indifferent, for one simply doesn't know
whence these traits come . . . as long as they are looked at
from the standpoint of the personal psychology of a single
earth-life.

Now I come back to the question: Where are the earlier
Initiates ? For certainly it will be said that they are not to be
found. But, my dear friends—I shall have to say something
paradoxical here !—if it were possible for a number of human
beings to be born to-day at the age of seventeen or eighteen,
so that when they descended from the spiritual world they
would in some way or other find and enter seventeen- or
eighteen-year-old bodies, or if at least human beings could
in some way be spared from going to school (as schools are

191

constituted to-day), then you would find that those who were once Initiates would be able to appear in the human being of the present day. But just as little as it is possible, under the conditions obtaining on earth to-day, for an Initiate, when he needs bread, to nourish himself from a piece of ice, just as little is it possible for the wisdom of an older time to manifest *directly*, in the form that you would expect, in a body that has received education—in the present-day accepted sense of the word—up to his seventeenth or eighteenth year. Nowhere in the world is this possible; at all events, nowhere in the civilised world. We have here to take account of things that lie altogether beyond the outlook of the educated men of modern times.

When, as is the custom to-day, a child is obliged as early as the sixth or seventh year to learn to read and write, it is torture for the soul that wants to develop and unfold in accordance with its own nature. I can only repeat what I have already told you in my autobiography, that I owe the removal of many hindrances to the circumstance that when I was twelve years old I was still unable to write properly. For the capacity of being able to write, in the way that is demanded to-day, kills certain qualities in the human being.

It is necessary to say such a thing, paradoxical though it may sound, for it is the truth. There is no help for it—it is a fact. Hence it is that a highly evolved individual can be recognised in his reincarnation only if one looks at manifestations of human nature which are not directly apparent *in* a man, if he has gone through a modern education, but reveal themselves, so to speak, *behind* him. We have in Garibaldi a most striking example of this. What did civilised men, including Cavour, or at all events the followers of Cavour, think of Garibaldi ? They regarded him as a madcap with whom it was useless to discuss anything in a sensible manner. That is a point of which we must take note; for there was much in his arguments and in his whole way of speaking that was bound to appear illogical, to say the least, to people enamoured of modern civilisation. Very often the things he says simply do not hold together. But when we are able to see behind a personality, and can look at that which in an earlier earth-life was able to enter into the body, but in *this* earth-life, because modern civilisation makes the bodies unfit, *was not able to enter into the body*—then we can begin to have an idea of what such a personality really is. Otherwise we are right off the track, for what is of most importance in such a personality lies right behind the things he can reveal externally. A good conventional man of the world, who simply expresses himself in the way he has learned to do, and in whom we see merely a reflection of the teaching and education he has received at school and elsewhere—such a man you can "photograph" in his moral and spiritual nature. He is there. A man, however, who comes over from other times bearing a soul filled with great and far-reaching wisdom, so that the soul cannot express itself in the body, can never be estimated with the means afforded by modern civilisation by what he does in the body. Above all, Garibaldi cannot be judged in that way. In his case it is rather like having to do—I am speaking metaphorically—with spiritualistic pictures, where a phantom becomes visible behind. With a personality like Garibaldi, you see him first as he is according to conventional standards, and behind you see something spiritual, a spirit-portrait, as it were, of that which in this incarnation cannot enter fully into the body.

When we take all this into consideration, and particularly if we meditate upon the special facts I have mentioned, then our vision is indeed led back from Garibaldi to a true Initiate who to all appearance lives out his Garibaldi-life in a quite different way, because he is unable to come down into his body.

If you consider the peculiar characteristics of Garibaldi's life to which I drew your attention, you will not find this so astonishing after all. A man must surely be somewhat of a stranger to earthly conventions if he finds his way into family relations through a telescope! Such a happening is certainly not usual, and it was not the only one in Garibaldi's life. In the characteristic style of his life there is something that

193

points right away from ordinary alignment with bourgeois conventions.

Thus, in the case of Garibaldi, we are led back to an Initiate-life, and it was a life in those Mysteries which I described to you some months ago as proceeding from Ireland. Garibaldi, however, is to be found in an offshoot of those Mysteries at no great distance from here, in Alsace. There we find him, as an Initiate of a certain degree. And it is moreover fairly certain that between this incarnation in the 9th century A.D., and his last incarnation in the 19th century, there was no further incarnation, but a long sojourn in the spiritual world. There you have the secret of this personality. He received all that I have described to you as the wisdom of Hibernia, and he received it at a very high stage of Initiation. He was within the places of the Mysteries in Ireland, and was actually the leader of the colony that came over later into Europe.

It goes without saying that just as an object reflected in a mirror becomes different in its reflected form, so all the wisdom of that time and place, embracing as it did the physical world and the spiritual world above it—all the wisdom in which an Initiate of those times participated, as I described it to you a few months ago—had to express itself during the 19th century in accordance with the civilisation of that period. You must accustom yourselves, when you find a philosopher in bygone times, or when you find a poet or an artist, *not* to look for the same individuality in the present epoch as a philosopher, poet or artist. The individuality passes from earth-life to earth-life, but the way in which he is able to live out his life depends upon what is possible in a particular epoch. Let me here insert an instance that will make this plain.

We will take another very well-known personality, *Ernst Haeckel*. Ernst Haeckel is famous as an enthusiastic adherent of a certain materialistic Monism—enthusiastic, one may say, to the point of fanaticism. He is well enough known to you; I need not give you any description of Haeckel. Now when we are led back from this personality to a former

194

incarnation, we come to Pope Gregory VII, the monk Hilde-brand, who afterwards became Pope Gregory VII.

I have chosen this instance so that you may see how differently the same individuality may express himself externally, in accordance with the cultural " climate " of the period. One would certainly not expect to look for the reincarnation of Pope Gregory VII in the 19th century representative of materialistic Monism.

The things that a man brings to manifestation on the physical plane, with the means afforded by external civilisa-tion, are far less important to the spiritual world than one is inclined to suppose. Behind the personalities of the monk Hildebrand and Haeckel lies something wherein they are alike and this is of much greater account than the differences between them. One of them fights to the utmost to enhance the power of Roman Catholicism, and the other fights to the utmost against Roman Catholicism, but for the spiritual world it makes little difference. These things, fundamentally speaking, are important for the physical world only; they are quite different from the underlying elements in human nature which count in the spiritual world. And so we need not be astonished, my dear friends, if we have to see in Garibaldi an Initiate from an earlier age, an Initiate, as I said, of the 9th century. In the 19th century this comes to expression in the only way possible during that century. You will agree that for the whole way in which a man takes his place in the world, his temperament, his qualities of character are of importance. But if everything that made up Garibaldi's soul in an earlier incarnation had emerged in the 19th century, together with his temperament, he would most certainly have been regarded as a lunatic by the men of the 19th century. He would have been considered quite mad. As much of him as could emerge—that, externally, was Garibaldi.

And now, once we have been led in a certain direction, explanations light up for other karmic connections. The other three men of whom I have spoken, who were brought together again with Garibaldi in one region and approxi-mately in the same decade, had been his pupils in that distant time—mark well, his *pupils*, assembled from distant parts of the earth, one from far away in the North, another from far away in the East and the third from far away in the West, called from all corners of the earth to be his pupils.

Now in the Irish Mysteries a definite obligation went with a certain degree of Initiation. It consisted in this, that the Initiate was bound to help on his pupils in all future earth-lives; he must not desert them. When, therefore, owing to their special karmic connections they make their appearance again on earth at the same time as their teacher, this means that he must experience the course of destiny with them; their karma has to be brought into reckoning with his own. If Garibaldi had not, at an earlier time, been associated as teacher with the individuality who came in Victor Emmanuel, then he would have been in very deed a Republican and would have founded the Republic of Italy. But behind all abstract principles are actual human lives passing from one earth-existence to another. Behind lies the duty of the Initiate of old towards his pupils. Hence the contradiction, for in accordance with the conceptions and ideas facing Garibaldi in the 19th century, he became quite naturally a Republican. What else should he have been ? I have known a number of Republicans who were faithful servants of royalty. Inwardly they were Republicans, for the simple reason that in a certain period of the 19th century—it is long past now, at the time when I was a boy—everyone who counted himself an intelligent person was a Republican. People said: Of course we are Republicans, only we must not show it in the outer world. Inwardly, however, they were Republicans. So, of course, was Garibaldi, except that he did not show it in the outer world. He did not carry his republicanism into effect and those who were inspired by him could not understand this. Why was it ? Because, as I have explained to you, he could not desert Victor Emmanuel, who was karmically united with him. He was obliged to help him on; and this was the only way he could do it.

Similarly the others, Cavour and Mazzini, were karmically united with Garibaldi, and he was able to do for them only as

196

much as their capacities allowed. Whatever could proceed from all four of them, that alone Garibaldi was able to bring to fulfilment. He could not go his own way independently.

From this deeply significant fact, my dear friends, you can see that many things in life can be explained only from out of an occult background.

Have you not often experienced how at some moment of his life a person does something that is quite incomprehensible to you? You would not have expected it of him; you cannot possibly explain it from his character. You feel that if he were to follow his personal character, he would do something different. And you may be right. But there is another man living near him, with whom he is karmically united, as in Garibaldi's case. Why does he act as he does? It is really only against an occult background that life becomes explicable. And so, in the case of Garibaldi, for example, we can truly say that we are led back to the Hibernian Mysteries—it sounds like a paradox but it is a fact. If we turn our gaze to the spiritual, we find that what meets us in external life on earth is, in many of its aspects, Maya. Many people with whom you are constantly together in ordinary life—if you could tell them what you are able to learn about them by looking through to the individuality behind—would be exceedingly astonished, they would be utterly bewildered. For what a man expresses outwardly—and this is particularly so in the present age, for the reasons I have given—is the merest fraction of what he really is, in terms of his former earth-lives. Many secrets are hidden in the things of which I am now speaking.

And now let us take the second personality of whom I gave you yesterday a brief characterisation—Lessing, who at the end of his life came forward with his pronouncement on repeated earth-lives. In his case we are led very far back, right back into Greek antiquity, when the ancient Mysteries of Greece were in their prime. Lessing was an Initiate in these Mysteries. And with him, too, we find that in the

18th century he was unable, so to speak, to come right down into his body. In the 13th century, as a repetition of his life in ancient Greece, we find an incarnation when he was a member of the Dominican Order, a distinguished Schoolman with subtle and penetrating concepts; and then, in the 18th century, he became the journalist par excellence of Middle Europe.

Take that drama of tolerance, *Nathan the Wise*, or such a book as *The Dramatic Art of Hamburg*—read for yourselves certain chapters of that book and then read *The Education of the Human Race*. These writings are comprehensible only on the assumption that all three incarnations of this personality have worked upon them: the Greek Initiate of olden times (read Lessing's treatise, *How the men of old pictured death*); the Schoolman, versed in medieval Aristotelianism; and lastly he who, with all this resting in his soul, found his way into the civilisation of the 18th century. Then, if you will keep in mind what I have just told you, a certain fact will become clear, a most striking and surprising fact.

It is remarkable how Lessing's life gives one the impression of a continual *search*. He himself brought this characteristic of his spiritual nature to expression when he uttered the famous saying, which has been quoted again and again (quoted, however, with very little understanding, by people who have no particular desire to strive after anything at all): " If God held in his right hand the whole full Truth, and in his left the everlasting striving after Truth, I would fall down before Him and say, ' Father, give me what thou hast in thy left hand '." A Lessing could say that. But when a mere pedant says it after him, it is of course intolerable. Lessing's whole life was indeed a search, an intense search. This comes to expression again and again in his works, and if we were honest with ourselves we should have to admit that many of Lessing's utterances are clumsy on this account, precisely those that are the most full of genius. People do not dare to admit that they stumble over them, because in history and literature Lessing is accounted a great man. In truth, however, his sayings often trip one up, so to speak; or, rather, they give one a feeling of being stabbed. You must, of course, become acquainted with Lessing himself to understand this. If you take up the book by Erich Schmidt, the two volumes on Lessing, then even when Erich Schmidt quotes him word for word you will not feel as though his utterances *impaled* you. Not at all! They may be the utterances of Lessing as far as the sound of the words goes, but what is written in the book before and after them takes away their edge.

It was not until the end of his earthly life that this seeker came to write *The Education of the Human Race*, which closes with the idea of repeated earth-lives. What is the explanation?

My dear friends, the way to understand this fact is through another fact I once mentioned. In the quarterly periodical*now discontinued, edited by our friend Bernus, I wrote an article on *The Chymical Wedding of Christian Rosenkreutz* and I drew attention to the fact that it was written down by a boy of seventeen or eighteen. The boy himself understood not a word of it. We have external proof of that. He wrote down this *Chymical Wedding* from beginning to end. The last page is not extant, but he wrote down the whole of the *Chymical Wedding*, without understanding a word of it. If he had understood it, he would have been bound to retain the understanding in later years. The boy, however, became a pastor, a good, honest pastor of the Württemberg-Swabian type, who wrote exhortations and theological treatises which are distinctly below the average, and very far indeed from having anything to do with the content of the *Chymical Wedding of Christian Rosenkreutz*. Life itself proves to us that it was not the Swabian pastor-to-be who wrote this *Chymical Wedding* out of his own soul. It is an inspired writing throughout.

So we may not always have to do with a man's own personality; there may be times when a spirit expresses itself through him. But there is a difference between the good Swabian pastor Valentin Andreae, who wrote those conventional theological treatises, and Lessing. Had Lessing

Das Reich. The articles are contained in the volume of the Complete Edition of Rudolf Steiner's works entitled, *Philosophie und Anthroposophie*. (Bibliographical No. 35.)

been Valentin Andreae, merely transported into the 18th century, he might perhaps have written in his youth a beautiful treatise on the Education of the Human Race, bringing in the idea of repeated earth-lives. But he was not Valentin Andreae; he was Lessing, Lessing who had no visions, who even—so it is said—had no dreams. He banished the inspirer—unconsciously of course. If the inspirer had wanted to take possession of him in his youth, Lessing would have said: Go away, I have nothing to do with you. He followed the path that was normal for an educated man in the 18th century. And so it was only in extreme old age that he was mature enough to understand what had been in him throughout his life. It was with him as it would have been with Valentin Andreae if the latter had also banished the inspirer, had written no trivial, edifying sermons and theological treatises, but had waited until he reached a grey old age and had then written the *Chymical Marriage of Christian Rosenkreutz* consciously.

Such are the links that unite successive earth-lives. And the day must come when this will be clearly understood. If we take a single earth-life, whether it be that of Goethe, or Lessing or Herbert Spencer or Shakespeare or Darwin, and look at what emerges from that life *alone*, it is just as though we were to pluck off a flower from a plant and imagine that it can exist by itself. A single life on earth is not comprehensible by itself; the explanation for it must be sought on the basis of repeated earth-lives.

And now we shall find it most interesting to study the two personalities of whom I spoke yesterday, Lord Byron and my geometry teacher. (You will pardon me if I become personal here.) They had in common only the construction of the foot, but this is a feature that specially repays attention. If one follows it up in an occult sense, it leads one to a peculiar condition of the *head* in an earlier earth-life. I have shown you a similar connection in the case of Eduard von Hartmann.—There is no getting over it. One can do no other than simply relate such things, as vision reveals them to one. No external, logical proofs, *no* proofs in the ordinary sense, can be given for these things.—When we follow the lives of these two men, it appears to us as though the lives they led in the 19th century had been shifted out of place. For we find, first of all, a contradiction of something mentioned here a few weeks ago—that in the course of certain cycles of time, those who were once contemporaries will incarnate again as contemporaries. Everything, of course, has its exceptions. In the spiritual world there are rules, but there are no rigid schemes. Everything is individual.

Thus in the case of these two personalities one is led back to a period when their lives ran together. I would never have found Byron in this earlier life if I had not found this geometry teacher of mine at his side. Byron was a genius. My geometry teacher was not even a genius in his own way. He was not a genius at all, but he was an excellent geometrician, quite the best I have ever come across, because he was a genuine geometrician and nothing else. In the case of a painter or a musician, you know that you are dealing with a one-sided man. For as a matter of fact, people are significant only when they are one-sided. As a rule, however, a geometrician in our time is not one-sided. A geometrician knows the whole of mathematics; when he constructs something in geometry, he always knows how to state the equations for it. He knows the mathematical, calculating side of it all. But this geometry teacher, though an excellent geometrician, was properly speaking no mathematician at all. He understood, for example, nothing whatever of analytical geometry. He knew nothing of the geometry that has to do with calculating and equations; in that respect he sometimes did the most childish things. On one occasion it was really very humorous. The man was so entirely a constructive geometrician and nothing else that he arrived by means of constructive geometry at the fact that the circle is the locus of the constant quotient. He found it out by construction, and since no one had found it before by construction, he regarded himself as its discoverer. We boys, who were as yet unsophisticated and had a good store of high spirits left in us, knew that in our book of analytical geometry it is shown how one sets up such and such an equation and the circle comes. We took the occasion to change the name of the circle and to start calling it by the name of our geometry teacher. The " N.N. line " we called it (I won't give his real name). This man had in fact the one-sidedness of the constructive geometrician to the point of genius. That was what was so significant about him; his character and talents were so clearly defined. People of the present day are not like that at all; you cannot get hold of them; they are like slippery eels! My teacher was anything but a slippery eel; he was a man with sharp corners, and that even in his external appearance. He had a face shaped like this—quite square, a most interesting head, absolutely four-angled, nowhere round. Really, you could study in the face of the man the right-angled nature of his peculiar constructive talent. It was most interesting.

Now, in vision, this personality is found directly by the side of Byron, and one is led back to early times in Eastern Europe, one or two hundred years before the Crusades. I once told you how, when the Roman Emperor Constantine founded Constantinople, he had the Palladium—which had been taken originally to Rome from Troy—removed from Rome to Constantinople. The transference was carried out with tremendous pomp and ceremony. For the Palladium was regarded as a particularly sacred object, which bestowed power upon whoever had it. It was firmly believed in Rome that as long as the Palladium lay beneath a pillar in the city, the power of Rome resided in it, and that this power had been brought across to Rome from the once mighty city of Troy, devastated by the Greeks. And so Constantine, whose destiny it was to transplant the power of Rome to Constantinople, caused the Palladium to be taken across to Constantinople with great pomp and ceremony, though to begin with, quite secretly. He caused it to be buried, a wall built about it, and set up an ancient pillar that came from Egypt, over the spot where the Palladium lay. On the top of the pillar he placed an ancient statue of Apollo, so arranged as to look like himself. Then he had nails brought from the Cross of Christ. And out of these he made a sort of halo for the statue, which was, as I have said, an ancient statue of Apollo and at the same time was supposed to represent himself. And so there the Palladium lay, in Constantinople.

Now there is a legend which has later assumed strange forms, but is in reality very, very ancient. Later, in connection with the Testament of Peter the Great, it was revived and transformed, but it goes back to very ancient times. The legend tells how at some time in the future the Palladium would leave Constantinople and come further up towards the North-East. Hence the idea in the Russia of a later time that the Palladium must be brought from the city of Constantinople into Russia, in order that all that is connected with the Palladium, and had been corrupted under the rule of the Turks, might have its place in the rule of Eastern Europe. Now these two personalities in olden times—it was one or two hundred years before the Crusades but I have not been able to fix the exact year—resolved to go out from what is now Russia to Constantinople in order, by some means or other, to capture the Palladium and bring it into the East of Europe.

They did not succeed. Such a project could never have succeeded, for the Palladium was well guarded. There was no possibility of getting hold of it, and those who knew how it was guarded were not to be won over. But an overwhelming pain took possession of these two men. And the pain that entered into them like a piercing ray, paralysing them both in the head, manifested in Lord Byron in his being somewhat like Achilles who was vulnerable in the heel, for Byron had a defect in his foot. On the other hand he was a genius in his head, which was a compensation for the paralysis he had suffered in that earlier earth-life. The other man also, on account of the paralysed head, had a defective foot, a club-foot. But let me tell you (for it is not generally realised) that man does not get geometry or mathematics out of his head. If you did not step the angle with your feet, your head would not have the perception of it. You would have no geometry at all if you did not walk and grasp hold of things. Geometry pushes its way up *through* the head and comes forth in ideas.

And in anyone who has a foot such as my geometry teacher had, there resides a strong capacity to be alive to the geometrical constitution of his limbs and his motor organism and to re-create it in his head.

If one penetrated more deeply into this geometry teacher of mine, into his whole spiritual configuration, one gained a significant impression of him as a human being. There was something really delightful about his way of doing things! Fundamentally speaking, he did *everything* from the point of view of a constructive geometrician and it was as if the rest of the world were simply not there. He was a singularly free human being, but one had only to observe him closely enough to feel as though some inner spell had once held sway over him and had brought him to the one-sided condition I have described.

But now in Lord Byron—I have mentioned the other man only because I should not have been able to get at the truth about Lord Byron if he had not put me on the track—in Lord Byron you can truly see karma working itself out. Once, long ago, he goes across from the East to fetch the Palladium. When he is born in the West, he goes eastward to help the cause of freedom, the spiritual Palladium of the 19th century. And he is drawn to the very same region of the earth to which he had gone long ago, from the other side. It is really staggering to see how the same individuality comes to the same locality in one life from one direction, in another life from another direction; first, attracted by something that is still deeply veiled in myth, and later by what had become the great ideal of the " age of enlightenment." There is something in all this that stirs one very deeply.

The things that come to light out of karmic connections are indeed startling. They always are. And in this realm we shall come to know of many other striking, paradoxical things. To-day I wanted to give you a grasp of the remarkable way in which the connections between earlier and later earth-lives can play into human existence.

COMPLETE EDITION

of the works of Rudolf Steiner in the original German. Published by the *Rudolf Steiner Nachlassverwaltung*, Dornach, Switzerland, by whom all rights are reserved.

General Plan (abbreviated):

A. WRITINGS

I. Works written between 1883 and 1925
II. Essays and articles written between 1882 and 1925
III. Letters, drafts, manuscripts, fragments, verses, inscriptions, meditative sayings, etc.

B. LECTURES

I. Public Lectures
II. Lectures to Members of the Anthroposophical Society on general anthroposophical subjects
   Lectures to Members on the history of the Anthroposophical Movement and Anthroposophical Society
III. Lectures and Courses on special branches of work:
   Art: Eurythmy, Speech and Drama, Music, Visual Arts, History of Art
   Education
   Medicine and Therapy
   Science
   Sociology and the Threefold Social Order
   Lectures given to Workmen at the Goetheanum

The total number of lectures amounts to some six thousand, shorthand reports of which are available in the case of the great majority.

C. REPRODUCTIONS and SKETCHES

Paintings in water colour, drawings, coloured diagrams, Eurythmy forms, etc.

When the Edition is complete the total number of volumes, each of a considerable size, will amount to several hundreds. A full and detailed *Bibliographical Survey*, with subjects, dates and places where the lectures were given, is available.

All the volumes can be obtained from the Rudolf Steiner Press in London as well as directly from the *Rudolf Steiner Nachlassverwaltung* (address as above).